Emergent Practice Planning

Emergent Practice Planning

Frances Ricks, Ph.D.

University of Victoria
Victoria, British Columbia, Canada

and

Jennifer Charlesworth

University of Victoria
Victoria, British Columbia, Canada

Kluwer Academic/Plenum Publishers
New York, Boston, Dordrecht, London, Moscow

ISBN HB: 0-306-47396-8
      PB: 0-306-47399-2

©2003 Kluwer Academic / Plenum Publishers, New York
233 Spring Street, New York, New York 10013

http://www.wkap.nl/

10 9 8 7 6 5 4 3 2 1

A C.I.P. record for this book is available from the Library of Congress

Preface

Emergent Practice Planning presents a new approach that challenges practitioners to deal with the complexity in case practice. It explores the interaction between the practitioner, context, planning, and acting. Effective case practice involves engaging in a process of inquiry and trial in order to assess, plan, and act. When we truly engage in inquiry and trial in practice we also emerge as practitioners. We emerge because the inquiry and trial process affects us as much as we influence it; the process is interactive. This interaction in practice accounts for new learning and personal change, and as we all know, new learning and personal change is easier said than done.

As we engage in this interactive process, new ideas about practice are formed. The challenge for all practitioners is to be aware and conscious of these new ideas about practice and the effects of these ideas on both the practitioner and practice. This consciousness is not easily achieved when our educational and work contexts suggest that there are "right answers" and that we should know what those are. In turn, we are expected to follow "the rules." This sets up the expectation that in practice there are "right ways" that are easy to learn and incorporate in practice.

We take a different view. After many years of practice as frontline practitioners, as researchers, and as trainers and educators of practitioners, we became aware of our continuous learning in practice and the importance of being able to reflect on personal change and its influence on practice. We also immersed ourselves in the research literature on self-awareness, reflective practice, change and how change works, and conducted our own research on mentoring, research in practice, community learning and practice, and caring in practice. What is apparent to us from our practice and research experiences is "many are the ways." Different approaches work for different people at different times.

Our learning was conclusive: **Nothing is conclusive**. Realizing and reflecting on this learning provided the genesis of this book. Rather than focus on what practitioners need to know in terms of knowledge, strategies, and clinical skills, we think that practitioners need to know that they do not know. Therefore, we place great importance on practitioners having the capacity to inquire and the skills of inquiry. The capacity to inquire and skills of inquiry can awaken new learning and consciousness within the constantly changing world of practice.

Emergent Practice Planning is an integrated framework requiring the practitioner to be awake and aware of what emerges in thinking or rethinking practice planning and how new thinking is manifested or evident in practice. Planning requires a formulation, a scheme, a detailed method by which something will be done. We are suggesting in this book that in order to plan, practitioners must be able to formulate and generate plans in light of their changing self, the people they are working with, and the changing context. This is no small task. Planning requires the capacity to think through what has been, what is now, and what might be. Can practitioners be prepared for emergent practice planning? We think so.

Emergent Practice Planning offers a nonstatic approach to thinking through practice and planning. First we engage the reader in identifying underlying assumptions for practice and urge continued reflection on assumptions throughout practice. Secondly we discuss the importance of language in practice, the need for models and frameworks, and the need for planning. We challenge the reader to be self-aware, to understand personal beliefs and values as a practitioner, to be able to articulate a theoretical orientation for change and how it works, and to be able to make discretionary judgments throughout the process of assessment, planning, and implementation of practice. Recognizing that practice occurs in context, models are offered to encourage thinking about different contexts. We also discuss how context adds complexity to practice. Finally, we discuss practice planning, planned change models, and case planning systems.

Emergent Practice Planning engages the frontline practitioner in discovering a lifestyle that involves being intentional, staying in inquiry, being reflective, having clarity of purpose and being willing to take action. In reading the book we expect practitioners to experience and reflect on their own emergence through personal learning and change while engaged in practice and practice planning.

Contents

1

Introduction

Key Themes: *There is a need for an alternative planning framework that takes into account the complexity of practice in these times and supports intentional practice and planning.*

Reflections: *As a supervisor in a child and family clinic in the early seventies, I noticed the lack of assessment and planning on the part of frontline workers. I became aware of the lack of assessment and planning curriculum in professional schools educating front-line workers in child and youth care, social work, nursing, and counseling practice. I wondered, Can practitioners work effectively with clients without negotiating a change plan with them? Are they able to deal with the complexity of practice without models and frameworks? Are practitioners able to be definitive in the moment, but still hold out for new ideas and new ways while providing service? What might that look like? Would organizations tolerate, never mind permit, discretionary judgments on the part of practitioners within defined standards and policy?*

> Each practice situation has its own time, place, or location, and circumstances that make it unique.

Players in Practice

This book is for all disciplines engaged in frontline work in health and social services. Disciplines are "collectives that include a large number and proportion of persons holding degrees with the same specialization name" (Weingart & Stehr, 2000). Disciplines represent some collective interests that correspond to a common intellectual interest and instructional tasks of a group of academics. Each discipline has its own body of knowledge and preferred ways of training and educating its members. Each discipline develops its own pedagogy and curriculum that is accredited by its respective professional organization.

This has been our history in professional development and education and dates back to the early 1900s.

We now live in an extraordinary time of knowledge. We know and can access more knowledge than ever before. What was once known by the elite is now known by every fourth grader. We are expected to know, we expect others to know, and we promote the acquisition of knowledge. We are "knowers," and our knowing was once bounded by our disciplines. No longer!

New ontological perspectives are evolving and emerging. For example, there is an awareness of unsuspected powers of the mind to mould "reality" rather than the other way around. The philosophy of physics is becoming indistinguishable from the philosophy of Buddhism, which is the philosophy of enlightenment. We are formulating reality as everything being unified and no longer as separate entities. What *is* may be beyond words, beyond concept, beyond form, perhaps even beyond time and space. This makes the journey of learning, or knowledge construction, quite a different journey. Perhaps on some days knowing may be out of our reach except at the level of some inner knowing that defies description and perhaps shared understanding.

We recognize the evolution that is taking place across disciplines as disciplines are engaging in interdisciplinary or multidisciplinary research and practice. However, in educational institutions we continue to hire social workers to train social workers and nurses to train nurses. We rarely take students from one discipline into another unless they go back and upgrade themselves in order to pursue our discipline's intellectual interests at a higher level. Meanwhile, in practice the disciplines are looking for collective interests that correspond to a common intellectual interest, and practices that go beyond previous disciplinary boundaries. This book offers a journey for all frontline workers who want to contemplate the theoretical and practical aspects of practice and practice planning, regardless of their disciplinary background.

Planning in Practice

In case planning and practice, we always work within a particular context. Each practice situation has its own time, place or location, and circumstances that make it unique. Just contemplating the different people involved in a practice situation can be challenging. For example, we may work with a child or youth who has a family and an extended family, as well as different service providers such as police, group-home workers, teachers, case supervisors, psychologists, social workers, family physicians, child and youth care workers, and perhaps others. All of those involved are members of larger systems that have their respective rules, regulations, values, and procedures for how things are supposed to proceed or be done.

We interact with all of these people and all of these larger systems, although our interactions may not always be direct. We may read a psychological report, talk to the teacher on the phone, or ask the group home for a report on the child's progress within the last month. We are more likely to interact directly with the child, family members, and those service providers who are immediately involved and at-hand. The others and their contexts are real and not real, present and not present, involved and not involved, depending on our awareness and capacity to relate to their contribution and influence.

This capacity to relate to different people's contributions and influences depends on who we are and what we know about ourselves. Individual practitioners have a set of belief systems that affect how they consider the situation, interact with other service providers, and respect and respond to the different rules, regulations, values, and procedures of various systems. Knowing about yourself as practitioner allows for greater understanding of why you do what you do and how that is separate from others with whom you are working.

As practitioners we are always in relation to these complex circumstances, and we are always engaged in multiple relationships within the context, whether we know it or not. In these complex circumstances there are many demands: to listen, to make astute observations, to problem-solve, and to be part of solutions that will change people, their lives, and their circumstances. We are expected to do this with grace, ease, and smiles on our faces because we are trained and know what to do—or think we should know what to do. This is like walking a tightrope over a deep crevice while balancing multiple relationships on our shoulders and head. If we do not know what to do, then what? If we make an error in judgment, is there any recourse? If we fall, will others fall with us? Have we failed?

> We need to be intentional about practice rather than perfect in practice.

We believe that as practitioners we need to be intentional about practice rather than perfect in practice. It is important to think about what we do in practice and why, to seek to know whether we are doing it well, and to learn as we go. In other words, practitioners not only need to be aware of what they do but also need to learn from falling—and not falling—into the crevice because it is part of the context.

The contextual aspects of case planning are not addressed in the contemporary case planning literature; instead, the approach is to jump right into case management and discuss steps, players, and tools. If context is discussed at all, it is restricted to discussing the utility of case planning and management in cost saving and service or resource utilization (Austin, 1990, 1993). A great deal of the contextual aspects of practice are either presumed or taken for granted.

In our view, this lack of contextual consciousness is one of the major challenges facing practitioners today. We feel a number of questions have not been addressed:

- How can we help practitioners appreciate the complexity of practice?
- How can we promote an appreciation of how the many aspects of practice are related?
- How can we engage practitioners in a learning process that will help them deal with the circular and untidy process of listening and observing, thinking, acting, and evaluating that is demanded moment by moment within practice?
- How can we help practitioners come to terms with what is perceived as failure and instead consider it a learning opportunity for future planning?

> For effective practice planning it is critical that practitioners understand that the complex nature of planning involves many choices and therefore many discretionary judgments.

We now realize that effective practice planning involves a constellation of models and frameworks that are used synergistically to influence practice and planning. Taken together, they shift and reform over time in an emergent way so that our practice and our planning at the case, service, program, and systems levels, changes. In *Emergent Practice Planning*, we make explicit what is often hidden and unavailable in discussions about practice planning. For example, for effective practice planning it is critical that practitioners understand that the complex nature of planning involves many choices and therefore many discretionary judgments. Ultimately it involves understanding what can or cannot be done in a particular situation, given the players involved and the resources at hand, and then weighing this carefully against what is needed and wanted.

Practice planning and plan execution is a complex process of decision making amidst current and multiple contexts. It is an iterative process of inquiry interspersed with choice-making among a set of perceived alternatives (see Figure 1.1). A choice at a point in time involves discretionary judgments on the part of practitioners, a process that can be enlightened through self-awareness and a greater understanding of frameworks, models, and interventions. Through self-awareness and greater understanding, more alternatives become apparent in practice.

Practitioners need to think through and understand the complexity of practice, the choices that confront them at every moment of practice, and the discretionary judgments they make every step of the way. *Emergent Practice Planning* is our effort to help practitioners define their practice process, including their practice-planning process that captures the case plan. We present an emergent practice planning framework that suggests aspects of practice requiring deliberation and intention on the part of practitioners. At the same time,

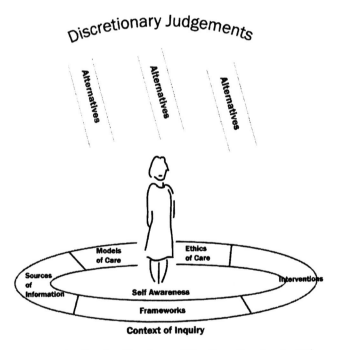

Figure 1.1.   Practice Planning and Plan Execution: Inquiry and
Discretionary Judgments.

the framework expects practitioners to maintain inquiry and to learn, grow, and change their practice through this process of inquiry. In other words, inquiry and growth foster a kind of practice that is emergent.

Emergent Practice Planning

Emergent practice planning is an integrated framework for understanding practice planning. It offers a new approach to conceptualizing critical aspects of practice and planning. Emergent refers to the process of inquiry that is the unifying thread throughout this book. Emergent is, by definition, a process for making things known through inquiry and trial. Practice refers to doing something or taking action. Planning introduces the idea that we act intentionally, with some purpose or objective in mind. Through planning and by being intentional in what we do, we are being more accountable for our actions. The process of emergent practice planning is easier said than done.

> Emergent is, by definition, a process for making things known through inquiry and trial.

> Emergent practice planning is a way of taking action according to some vision and sense of direction, in order to affect both change *and* learning as we proceed so that subsequent action is informed by the learning.

Emergent practice planning is our attempt to describe a way of thinking and doing that is a way of taking action according to some vision and sense of direction in order to affect both change and learning as we proceed, so that subsequent action is informed by the learning. Metaphorically, it is a wave in the ocean. Although the wave changes, shifts, and takes different forms as the conditions require or dictate, it continues forward into the shore.

The domain for emergent practice planning (EPP) is mapped out as follows: emergent-self as practitioner, the context for practice, and planning. Central to the EPP framework is the practitioners' intention in practice to pose constant choice throughout EPP (see Figure 1.2). Each aspect of the framework relates to a critical aspect of the practice planning process.

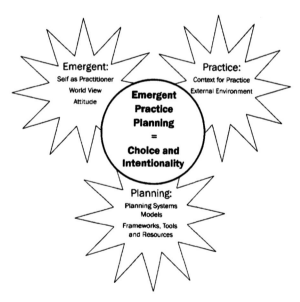

Figure 1.2. Emergent Practice Planning (EPP) Framework.

1. *Emergent-self as practitioner* points out that practitioners must have an understanding of self and that practice emerges out of personal beliefs and values. This

section asks you to reflect on your interacting and engaging self and to be aware of your evolving self in relation to being an intentional practitioner in relationships with others.

2. *Context for practice* outlines the need to understand how different aspects of the environment interrelate and affect your practice.

3. *Planning* involves noting your intentions with regard to practice. It is designed to have you consider the extent to which you deliberately reflect on and make decisions aimed at prompting or promoting change.

4. *Choice* focuses your attention on being a self-determining practitioner. You are asked to explore the limitations of freedom and autonomy in light of your beliefs and values and the constraints of your practice contexts.

Case Study: Susan is an inexperienced worker at an interdisciplinary outpatient clinic for families. She has taken over an existing case load of 36 families that are culturally divergent. There is no specified supervision, no written guidelines for case planning, and few meetings. Basically she is on her own. Her thoughts emerge as she struggles to define the nature of her work, and her questions parallel aspects of the EPP framework. "I thought I knew what I was doing. I don't have a clue. Most of these families have children and I can't imagine some of the problems they are reporting. How could things get this bad? This challenges what I thought about families. I am not sure that these families can change. Change what, I wonder? Clearly these families are not like mine! And where is everyone? I have no one to talk to; no one has told me about the other agencies involved with these clients. I don't know where to begin. Seems like there should be something in the files but all I can find are loose notes that are in no particular order. What a mess!

Seven underlying assumptions: (a) People can change and practitioners can help in the change process; (b) The practitioner is instrumental in making a difference in people's lives; (c) The relationship between the practitioner and the client, and the client's circumstances and issues, are context dependent; (d) The change relationship is a mutual journey of inquiry and learning; (e) If you give people a healthy alternative, they will take it every time; (f) Our best will not always be enough unless we learn from it; and (g) Many are the ways ... there is more than one best practice.

On your pathway to being and becoming an emergent practitioner, use this framework to reflect on and rethink your experiences and point of view. Your practice planning—and how you work with others—will change as you have different experiences in different systems, as you read different theories, and as you add to your strategies for assessment and intervention. You can revisit the framework many times and remember that you are engaged in an ongoing process of emergent practice planning.

Underlying Assumptions

There are seven core assumptions underlying how one works from the EPP perspective. It is important for practitioners to have clear practice assumptions because these define their fundamental views of practice and guide how their practice is conducted. It may be helpful for you to consider the core assumptions listed below and reflect upon how much you share, or do not share, them.

1. *People can change and practitioners can help in the change process.*
   The change process takes place within a relationship where there is an explicit contract to change. This assumption defines the purpose of practice—that is, to participate in a relationship in a way that makes a difference in the lives of others. This purpose is known and understood by practitioners and clients.

2. *The practitioner is instrumental in making a difference in people's lives.*
   Although people can and do initiate and promote their own change process, in the change-process relationship the practitioner's role is to be intentional in prompting the change. Things change around us all the time. Sometimes, if we wait the problem changes or simply goes away. Other times, there are happy accidents—for example, we do something that turns out to be therapeutic or promotes change in others. It can be quite unintentional and yet years later people will report that what you said or did changed their lives forever. These are wonderful change experiences, but they are not the same as being in a situation where the practitioner intentionally participates to promote or prompt change.

3. *The relationship between the practitioner and the client, and the client's circumstances and issues, are context dependent.*

   > The change-process relationship is part of the context of change.

   The change-process relationship is part of the context of change. The client's problem or issue occurs within an environment where certain circumstances and forces are at work. In other words, the context is one of the frames for understanding the issue and what sustains it. Changes to be addressed must be considered in terms of other people and forces within the client's environment, whatever they might be. Practice that occurs in isolation or without consideration of the larger context and circumstances will not survive the test of time because context factors are related to and impinge on the nature and resolution of the issues.

4. *The change relationship is a mutual journey of inquiry and learning.*

   > Change is possible only through inquiry and learning, because you cannot change what you do not know or understand.

   The practitioner and client create and engage in a relationship of mutual respect that allows them to understand and to know each other. Clients inform practitioners of their understanding of their issues, and practitioners share novel perspectives and opportunities that create windows for change. Change is possible only through inquiry and learning, because you cannot change what you do not know or understand. The choices within the relationship are usually mutually determined.

5. *If you give people a healthy alternative, they will take it every time.*

   > Given the opportunity to see, understand, and learn new ways, they will take up change, sometimes with pain and other times with joy in their hearts.

   The challenge for creating change is to open up real options to the client. If they are drinking, participating in violence, not caring for their children, attempting suicide, or engaging in any other defeating behaviors or activities, it is because they either see no harm or know no other way to address the issue. Given the opportunity to see, understand, and learn new ways, they will take up change—sometimes with pain and other times with joy in their hearts.

6. *Our best will not always be enough unless we learn from it.*
   In the past 100 years, great advances in medicine and other human services have occurred, accompanied by social expectations that practitioners can fix anything. Success, as well as failure, comes through inquiry and trial, but it is often not a quick or satisfactory solution. Practitioners striving for perfection must come to terms with doing their best and sometimes failing. The challenge is to understand and document the limitations that may intrude on desired results or outcomes while getting on with the next trial.

7. *Many are the ways... there is more than one way to practice.*
   Recent research on theoretical practice models (Prochaska, Norcross, & DiClemente, 1994) revealed that different approaches share common processes. These include:

- Consciousness raising: increasing information about the self and the problem
- Social liberation: increasing social alternatives for behaviors that are not problematic
- Emotional arousal: experiencing and expressing feelings about one's problems and solutions
- Self re-evaluation: assessing feelings and thoughts about self with respect to the problem
- Commitment: choosing and committing to act, or belief in ability to change
- Countering: substituting alternatives for problem behaviors
- Environment control: avoiding stimuli that elicit problem behaviors
- Reward: rewarding self or being rewarded for changing and helping relationships and enlisting the help of someone who cares.

> Practitioners from different theoretical orientations use similar process strategies to achieve similar goals in their work.

In other words, practitioners from different theoretical orientations use similar process strategies to achieve similar goals in their work. They may use different words to express what they are doing, but the meaning of what they are doing is the same.

These seven assumptions, or fundamental beliefs, influence how we view practice and are reflected throughout this book. For example, we present different theoretical orientations for practice and suggest that it does not matter which one or ones you use, as long as you have one or more to guide what you do. Our position reflects our assumption that there is more than one best practice. Although we firmly believe that practitioners are instrumental in making a difference in people's lives, we also believe that all practitioners need a theoretical orientation and planned-change model in order to be intentional and deliberate in their work. The change relationship as a "mutual journey of inquiry and learning" is probably the most basic

> The change relationship as a "mutual journey of inquiry and learning" is probably the most basic assumption of the book.

assumption of the book. Inquiry and learning, and the processes for them, are presented throughout in the belief that change is a function of inquiry and learning on the part of practitioners and clients.

If you find yourself disagreeing with some of our ideas, consider the possibility that it may be related to one of our assumptions rather than a particular topic or idea. Sometimes our assumptions are so embedded in our thinking that we no longer recognize them as important manifestations of who we are.

Where to Start?

As we began writing this book, we realized that we could start in any number of different places. Why? Because the book, like the subject we are addressing, is emerging. Neither stable nor static, it is evolving, fluid, and, in many ways, not definable; yet it can be defined at a particular moment.

At times we wondered whether this book could be written because, as soon as we wrote it, things would change. We had a choice. We could throw up our hands in despair on the theory that practice in the health and social service fields cannot be articulated due to its ever-changing nature. Alternatively, we could take a position that, while practice and planning are emergent and therefore not definable, processes for facilitating better and continuous understanding of both practice and planning do exist. Clearly we have chosen to do the latter. This book is about practice and practice planning. More specifically, it is about:

- Thinking about what we do in practice and why
- Knowing whether we are doing it well
- Learning as we go how to do it differently
- Coming to terms with failure while emerging.

We encourage you to work with the material presented here to add to your own journey of thinking, knowing, and learning about practice and being a practitioner in these times. We seek to present practical and usable frameworks, models, and techniques that may be relevant to you as a health and social services practitioner. However, this is not a "how to" book; after all, practice is emergent. Recognizing this, we engage you in a process of reflection—about yourself and about the context within which you live and practice—and encourage you to stay open to different points of view, new material, and personal discomfort. We invite you to rethink your practice, how you manage or plan your cases, and the way in which you generate case plans.

2

Setting the Stage

Key Themes: *EPP is a practice lifestyle that involves being intentional, staying in inquiry, being reflective, having clarity of purpose, and being willing to take action.*

Reflections: *When I first began my career as a child and youth care worker, I thought that practice in the health and social services field was about getting busy and making things better. I knew a little about case planning and that periodically I would be expected to generate case plans, but for me planning was separate and apart from my world of practice. At times, I viewed the plans that were in place as constraints to my practice. Indeed, given how and why these plans were created, they probably were constraining and irrelevant. However, I have come to appreciate the interconnectedness of practice and planning. I have also come to realize that this integration of practice and planning takes place within multifaceted and complex contexts. In my current practice, I think and reflect more; I ask more questions. I am not as afraid to say, "I don't know," and I ask others—particularly clients—for their perspective. Some of my questions are: What can we learn from our mistakes? What should I do with people who expect me to be an expert and the doer? How can we be creative, intentional, and effective in a way that works for all of us?*

The Nature of Practice

Thinking about practice requires reflection on the ontological aspects, or the nature of, practice. What do we mean by practice? How do we represent what we mean in language? Can practice be captured in frameworks and models? Why use them? What are the key aspects of practice? In this section, we discuss these and other aspects of practice to prompt your thinking about the nature of practice and how to represent it.

Language and Meaning

We frequently find ourselves challenged to communicate complex ideas through the written word. The written language is both limited and loaded. It is limited in the sense that the richness of communication achieved through nonverbal, experiential, and dialogic means cannot be replicated in text. Written language is loaded because many words are associated with particular ways of thinking and points of view. Definitions are both granted and denied by practitioners of various stripes and colors. Assumptions about people and situations are often made on the basis of the language used, thus either including or excluding people and ideas. Oftentimes, words are used with no intention to include or exclude, but nonetheless, this is the effect.

A good example is the use of the word "client." Notice your assumptions about the meaning of the word. Notice your assumptions about the meaning of other words that represent client, such as participant or patient. More to the point, notice your judgments about people who use the word "client."

Language is not only limited and loaded, but it also changes as words take on new meaning in different contexts and over time. In fact, as new ideas are expressed and articulated, new words emerge. One of the challenges we faced in writing this book and in our own practice was having to confront the paradox of using words that have meaning in the dictionary while changing in meaning as we use them. It is therefore important that we reflect on the study of language and the implications for understanding and representing the reality of practice.

The study of meaning in language is both defined and elusive in terms of how it represents our reality. For example, Steven Friedman (1993) has offered the following four views of language:

1. *A common sense view of language is that language is transparent and true.*
    In this view, the use of language is an expression of already existing facts. This view assumes that we are able to perceive the truth of reality, and equally able to express our experience of this reality through language. This makes it possible for readers and listeners to know exactly what we mean.
2. *The traditional Western view of language is that language can and does represent reality.*
    This view is also based on the assumption that there is a reality to be represented and that language can represent it. From this point of view, meaning can be developed by either looking behind and beneath the words or by going into the structure of language. This requires going beyond the surface of the meaning of words.
3. *Buddhists argue that language blocks access to reality.*
    Although they too think there is a reality out there, they use the practice of meditation to "turn off" language. They consider language to be an obstruction to accessing reality.
4. *Poststructuralism posits that language is reality.*
    Meaning is derived through negotiation within a specific context, during which messages are sent and received. Therefore, what gets talked about—and how it gets talked about—makes a difference in terms of the reality. In effect, reality is a subjective and contextual experience as it is being created or constructed within the dialogue.

These are important formulations about the nature of language, not because they are true, but because they demonstrate quite clearly that the world of language, as well as language itself, is changing. Are our theoretical views of language shifting because our view of what reality is, and what represents reality, is changing? Are we faced with the chicken-and-egg which-came-first question? Or, is it even more complex?

These are important formulations about the nature of language, not because they are true, but because they demonstrate quite clearly that the world of language, as well as language itself, is changing.

This changing view of language presents interesting language challenges about practice, both in these times and in this book. Poststructuralists challenge our use of words such as problem, solution, clients, case load, and managing, arguing that the use of such words takes us on a certain pathway and forges the reality in which we begin to operate. For example, the use of the word "problem" poses the need for a solution, while "client" poses the need for a practitioner or helper, and "case manager" poses the need for someone to do the managing. Given this kind of thinking, everything needs to be negotiated within the particular context and by the players involved. Nothing is taken for granted, and nothing is assumed about the meaning of what is being said; the meaning will be created through the language exchange and interaction of participants.

There is a certain paradox in the attempt to capture the fluidity of reality as represented by the process of languaging. The paradox is the emergence of "language cops" within groups holding certain views about the use of language. Some people, for instance, advocate for more inclusion of others, acceptance of diversity, and more respect for difference. They consider the lack of inclusion, acceptance, and respect as being a function of the power structure that has long been represented by the hierarchy and patriarchy. In their quest, they have claimed ownership of certain words, defining them within their particular theoretical perspective. Thus, some words have come to have a specific and narrow meaning, while the use of others is decried as offensive, wrong, or at least politically incorrect.

A key example is the use of the word "power." Power has come to mean "power over," which is actually the dictionary definition of the word "authority." There are several popular assumptions about the word, including power corrupts, power is abusive, experts have power, and there is personal and institutional power. This is interesting in light of the dictionary definition of "power", which is "to act or to do." If we act or do something, we are asserting our power.

Perhaps the idea of abuse of power is related more to the current assumptions about power rather than its nominal definition. Perhaps these assumptions have emerged and a new definition of power is emerging in these times and within certain contexts. Perhaps abuse of power will come to be defined as someone doing something we don't like, or what we interpret to be an assertion of power over someone. The point is that "power over" is relative to having "authority over," and it appears to be taking on new meaning. As an illustration, consider the meaning of power in the context of providing care (see Figure 2.1). This offers a different perspective on what power could mean, depending on the context, and how important it is to understand the context of the use of words.

This word "power" is very popular in critical theory, feminist theory, and other perspectives that are concerned with matters of equity. Clients are viewed as people who have been marginalized by those with power. Not surprisingly, proponents of this view argue that we must do away with power, as well as the use of the word "client," in order to do

In the context of providing care, I have the power to...

- make a difference
- change and change processes
- embark on a mutual journey of inquiry and learning
- be inclusive
- choose healthy alternatives

Figure 2.1. Power in the Context of Care.

Let's offer practitioners the option of using words that have certain accepted definitions or that can be defined within a particular context.

away with marginalization. Although we would agree that many clients are marginalized, this can be explained in any number of ways depending on the context and the situation—power over being one of them.

The meaning-of-language phenomenon is very evident in the world of practice. As we struggle with being more relative and inclusive about our views of what is and what to do in practice, we also struggle with how to express what is and what to do. At the very least we concede that "what is" could change tomorrow. At the very worst we insist that certain words, like those mentioned earlier, must not be used. We deem them categorically inappropriate because they mean certain things and take us down certain pathways of practice as if they own us.

To us the real language challenge is not to throw out certain words because we fear they might negatively influence practice, or may have in the past. Instead, let's offer practitioners the option of using words that have certain accepted definitions or that can be defined within a particular context. For example, "client" means a user of professional services. Professional services are those services for which we get paid. "Goal" means the object of effort; therefore, client goals would be statements of client-desired change and where we would put our efforts. "Case," in relation to work (as in case work), refers to the individuals, groups, families, or communities that we are concerned with as cases. "Management," as it pertains to clients, means the technique of treatment, and treatment means the mode or way of dealing with, or behaving towards, a person.

Another important point is that words in the dictionary have definitions for word contexts. For example, "goal" has different meanings in the context of a game. In the context of a game, either it means a point marking the end of a game, or, if one attempts to kick a goal, it means a line between two posts. This is an interesting and subtle aspect of defined language; there is usually more than one definition for a word and that definition is affected by how the word is used—for example, as noun or verb—as well as the context in which the word appears or is used.

Dictionaries explain the words of a language. They thus serve as guides within language groups, providing the shared meaning and use of particular words; we often refer to them for the correct spelling of a word. However, what the four views of language make evident are the ever-evolving aspects of language in terms of ontological views (nature of reality) and definitions of words. We may, in fact, be moving away from dictionaries because we experience them as another form of social control. Certainly some theorists decry the use of American Psychological Association guidelines for professional writing and instead promote finding your voice in your own format. Would this be evidence of creating a different writing and communication reality in poststructuralist times?

Notice that none of the definitions for the practice words mentioned above represents our worst fears about practice; that is, as practitioners, we will take control, we will be in charge, we will have power over, we will marginalize our clients, and because we refer to them as clients, we will relate to them as objects in a cold and impersonal way. How we work with clients in practice is more likely to depend on our fundamental beliefs and assumptions about people, change, practitioners, health, what matters and what doesn't, and what works and what doesn't. Perhaps our discussions should focus on these weightier matters as we find our way in the world of practice, which is, and has been for some time, a never-ending story.

In summary then, please don't get "hooked" by the language that we use, but do reflect on it. We seek neither to create another vocabulary nor to align with or distance ourselves from the practice vocabulary already in use. Words are the best tools we have for conveying ideas that have meaning to us, but they are still just words. We have done our best to use them to present some ideas and practices that are often not easy to put into words. We urge you to consider the language used in this book and compare it with the language you use in defining practice.

Models, Frameworks, and Other Ideas

This book has its roots in our observations of exceptional practice, where we noticed practitioners working simultaneously and synergistically with multiple models and frameworks. The book, therefore, has evolved into a collection of multiple models and frameworks. We believe practitioners use a myriad of frameworks to develop an understanding about what they do, why they do it, what effect it has, and what they can learn that will inform their practice and planning—in other words, thinking, knowing, and learning. Before we launch into an overview of frameworks and models, we want to present our view about frameworks, models, and their benefits and limitations.

> Frameworks are representations of the essential parts of something.

Frameworks are representations of the essential parts of something. For example, a house frame represents the outside parameters of a house structure, as well as the rooms in relation to each other. A model is more complex than a framework. It is a description of the parts of the whole, representing the working relationship of the parts as well as the calculations needed to put the model together. In our example of the house, the frame is the structure that represents the outside and the rooms. The model is the blueprint that is used to put the house together according to certain specifications. Neither the frame nor the model can (or claim to) capture what it will be like to live within the house, what furnishings will be put where, how people will react to the space, or how people will live within the house. However, both are helpful in identifying what the intention is and what needs to be taken into account in the creation of the house space.

Models and frameworks have both benefits and limitations in health and social services work. In the benefits column, they

- Guide thinking, offering a focus for inquiry and reflection
- Provide an overview of the topic, including different aspects, or parts, under consideration

- Provide categories to organize information
- Establish a shared understanding between people and teams working with a particular model, including the clients
- Guide practice, making practice more deliberate and intentional.

To be intentional in practice, practitioners need practice frameworks and models, or ways of thinking about critical aspects of practice and how each aspect works or unfolds, or works in relation to the others. Models and frameworks help identify and define different aspects of practice; they can then be used to organize our data collection and our thinking and planning of what to do within each critical aspect of practice. Ultimately, they affect how we do what we do.

However, these benefits are tempered by limitations. Models and frameworks

- Are reductionistic, therefore simplistic
- Are subject to wide interpretation
- Can be misused to prescribe rather than guide practice
- Are seen as proxies for competency.

In seeking to distill complex phenomena into a simpler and more understandable form, models and frameworks often fragment, reduce, and isolate phenomena such that the integrity of the whole is lost. They capture the essence of, but never the whole of, something, and what they do capture of the whole is often necessarily sparse or bare bones. Although the bare bones can be useful in suggesting a map of the territory or the essence of what is being framed, they should not be assumed either to represent all there is to know and understand about aspects of a practice or to represent or dictate what steps to take in conducting one's practice.

> "For every complex problem, there is a simple solution that is elegant, easy to understand and wrong." (H.L. Mencken)

From years of working with case-planning models in our own practice, and encouraging their use in the practice of others (Ricks, 1991), it became clear to us that case-management models are all too often embraced as linear, lock-step frameworks. Although these frameworks were not intended to be embraced as linear models, they were, and still are, often applied in a reductionistic way. They focus on identifying (isolating) the problem, deciding what contributed to it and what should be done about it, and then taking specific action. The underlying premise accompanying these frameworks and models seems to be: If we can just figure out the problem (or specify the right goal, or find the right action), then we will be managing and things will get better.

In effect, the application of such models defines practice rather than representing the case plan for a particular context of practice planning. The reality was (and is) that this way of thinking and practicing serves neither the client nor the practitioner in the long run. Understandably, a contingent of practitioners reacted to what they understood to be a reductionistic approach and presumed that the source of the problem lay with the articulation of models and frameworks. However, we believe that the problem lies not so much with the notion of models and frameworks, but with their interpretation and application. Too often they are seen as the answer, which they can never be.

Case-management frameworks contain the essential elements of what we want described, understood, and explained about a case. They fall short of capturing everything because frameworks are designed to communicate only the key aspects of a case; a more inclusive approach to practice would incorporate all activities of providing service and might include policies and procedures, intake, assessment, case conferencing for overall goal setting and service planning, case conferencing for program goal setting and service planning, and evaluation. Further, roles might be outlined and defined to ensure that everyone knows who carries what responsibility and how practitioners are supposed to work together.

The challenge in presenting frameworks and models is that the interpretation and application of them is in the hands of the practitioner. For example, models have been criticized by some as being *deficit* models, because they fail to consider personal strengths and only focus on what is missing. However, given some people's use of these models in practice, nothing could be further from the truth. It would be impossible to discover what is missing without considering what is not missing or personal strengths! Clearly, it depends on how the practitioner uses the model.

Another limitation from our perspective is that the model or framework may be embraced as a prescription for action, as "this is the way you have to do it." However, practitioners can use frameworks and models simply to guide their thinking; the use of them may shape or point to a process, but it does not dictate or prescribe a process. Certainly, they cannot spell out every little step that must be taken in practice. We have also noticed that sometimes frameworks and models are imbued with a sense of "If you accept this model, you must practice in a specific way." We suggest that the purpose of frameworks and models depends on the practitioner. In EPP, we think they are valuable tools to be used when thinking through, planning, and conducting one's practice.

Models and frameworks do not ensure competent practice, although we have noticed that they are often presented as being capable of doing so. Frameworks and models are not designed to ensure competency. Competency is assured by hiring competent people who can use models and frameworks. To put it bluntly, competent people make models and frameworks and then make them work. Models and frameworks do not make people competent and do not dictate what must be done.

> Competency is assured by hiring competent people who can use models and frameworks.

The frameworks and models presented in this book are intended to prompt your thinking and to offer a focus for reflection. Implied in each aspect of each framework is "think about this." Keep in mind that you are responsible for doing the thinking and for determining what you will and will not incorporate in your practice planning framework and process.

Using the Emergent Practice Planning Framework

The Emergent Practice Planning (EPP) framework urges practitioners to select or create models that work for them. We provide examples of frameworks and models that could be used to guide inquiry, thinking, and planning within practice. The purpose of the EPP framework and the models is to prompt practitioners to first examine

> The purpose of the EPP framework and the models is to prompt practitioners to first examine their own practice frameworks and models, and then create, reconstruct, or maintain them.

their own practice frameworks and models, and then create, reconstruct, or maintain them. What we offer is an attitude, along with useful and time-tested models and processes that may, when combined with your knowledge, skill, understanding, and perspective, bring about a meaningful and effective practice.

Although many models and frameworks are presented in this book, they are not the only ones that could be useful to you. Also, please consider all of them, as they are offered for your consideration, analysis, and trial. Each has benefits and limitations, which we seek to identify. More important, underlying the frameworks and models that we present are our beliefs about the areas of practice that require them. In other words, whether or not you use the frameworks as presented is not as important as recognizing the need for frameworks, or ways of thinking, for critical aspects of practice. The frameworks and models presented here reflect the four elements of the EPP framework:

- Emergent-self as practitioner
- Context for practice
- Planning (and decision making)
- Choice (and intentionality).

The EPP framework emphasizes the discretionary nature of practice and how it relates to the practitioner, the context for practice, and decision making and planning. Practitioners have the liberty of deciding (as they see fit or within limits) about what to do. To make discretionary judgments, practitioners need to understand the four elements of EPP as aspects of practice that they affect through momentary judgments. This assumes, we suggest, that practitioners are fit to manage practice. We ask you to consider the following four aspects of practice in developing and evolving your practice.

Emergent-Self as Practitioner

Key to understanding self as practitioner is recognizing what matters to you in life and how that is related to being motivated to work with and for others. Is practice about making the world a better place? Is it about helping others and being recognized and appreciated for doing that? Is it because being a practitioner offers a forum for working out your own issues? Is it a combination of these and other reasons?

> The self and the practitioner are one and the same. Without the self there is no practitioner.

What becomes very clear in addressing these questions is that the self and the practitioner are one and the same. Without the self there is no practitioner. Further, without the self there is no other. It is through the self or from the self that one's practice is defined, becomes, and evolves. It is through the self that purpose and intentions for practice are manifested. The self-definition and our awareness of it evolves in relationship to others across contexts of home, school, and community. Therefore, knowing the "interacting" self and being aware of the evolving self are critical to being an intentional practitioner and to being in relationship with others.

How you define practice will be shaped, driven, or affected by what you want to achieve and create—that is, your purpose in practice. Your beliefs and values about change and how change works will be related to your purpose and your definitions of practice. These fundamental beliefs and values will be more or less congruent with certain theoretical orientations, which have their own embedded beliefs and values. Because these beliefs and values guide your use of techniques and methods, if you watch yourself closely in practice, you will notice inconsistencies and incongruencies. A closely-watched practice can reveal how your "theory-in-use" is evolving. You may see your strengths and limitations reflected in the use of certain theoretical orientations and methodologies, or you may discover how you engage with others in seeking and giving support in relationships.

> A closely watched practice can reveal how your "theory-in-use" is evolving.

Only by recognizing and embracing the self as practitioner and by being willing to engage in a process of inquiry and trial about the self as practitioner, can you learn and evolve throughout your practice or with practice (pun intended).

Context for Practice

> The context of practice influences practice. Where you work gives focus to the work.

The context of practice influences practice. Where you work gives focus to the work. For example, the work in a private clinic is different from that in a group home or community center. The nature of the organization and service settings affects practice. Some organizations promote change through advocacy while others promote change through education. Some work settings prescribe hours of work, number of clients, theoretical orientations, assessment methods to be used, policies and procedures for living circumstances, and so on. It is important to understand how different aspects of the environment interrelate and affect your practice. Understanding how compatible and congruent the context of practice is with your model of care is critical to working within any environment. How effective are you in this model of care? How does your work environment affect your practice? How do others work with you and how does that affect you? Are you being driven by the environment to operate in ways that violate your code of conduct as a practitioner? Is there anything you can do? If not, why not?

Planning

Planning distinguishes the unintentional practitioner from the intentional practitioner. "Ready, fire, aim" is an old joke, but it makes the point. If you do not READY yourself by conducting assessments, if you do not AIM by defining goals or deciding where you and your client are headed, then when you FIRE by taking specific actions, chances are you will miss the target. There are fundamental positions that affect how you get ready, how you aim, and when you fire. What is your position on change and how do you think it works? What is the role of the practitioner with regard to change? Is assessment, planning, and decision making relevant to the change process? Do you take an active or passive role in the change process? Do you take a therapeutic or educational approach? Do you make a distinction between change through therapeutic interventions and educational strategies?

What is your position on the use of frameworks and models for assessment, decision making, and planning for change? Do you have a model or framework for assessment, decision making, and planning for change? What do you take into account as you plan, who do you engage or collaborate with, what is your objective through planning, and what are the criteria you use to make decisions? Why these particular criteria? Do you even know?

Choice

Our presumption in using choice as our fourth aspect of practice is that we are self-determining beings. In other words, as practitioners we have freedom and autonomy. This poses the question of what we have freedom and autonomy to do, and we suggest the answer is to determine the self as practitioner—that is, to determine what kind of person and practitioner you will be.

> To be a practitioner in current practice contexts requires an appreciation of how your practice emerges through an interactive process within the context.

It has been suggested that "complete" choice is not possible because it is impossible to access all the information needed to access all options. This is an important idea as it points to the need for you to understand what you have, and do not have, choice over. The cultural context of practice in fact limits your choices. To be a practitioner in current practice contexts requires an appreciation of how your practice emerges through an interactive process within the context. This means that practice is not totally determined by the self independently, but rather by the self interacting with others in an interdependent way.

> Through every step of practice, you are engaged with clients in an interactive process of deciding or choosing whether to work together, what the problem is and what it means, how the circumstances and the person could be different, what steps to take to bring about change, and how to know whether it worked.

Now consider what this would look like throughout the practice process. Through every step of practice, you are engaged with clients in an interactive process of

- Deciding or choosing whether to work together
- What the problem is and what it means
- How the circumstances and the person could be different
- What steps to take to bring about change
- How to know whether it worked.

Each step has contextual or cultural constraints imposed on the choices that come up every moment, for everyone involved. These constraints may be in the form of the information you get or do not get, the requirements of professional associations, the demands of the work environment, and people's different preferences. Practitioners are challenged to come to terms with choice as it confronts them at every moment of their practice.

These four aspects of practice or frames, clustered together, form the basis for EPP. Each of these frames is emergent; the frames together are both synergistic and emergent. The emergent quality of each frame that we hold, as well as the cluster of frames, can be developed and informed by a number of different processes, information sources, and other frameworks and models. They can be developed and informed through personal reflection, through dialogue with others, and through research evidence, to name but a few.

To help you rethink your practice and consider how these various frames are interconnected, we offer Figure 2.2, where the emergent process is viewed as being within a mutual Culture of Inquiry (Ricks, Charlesworth, Bellefeuille, & Field, 1999). In this culture of inquiry, there is a process of listening, process-ing, integrating, and understanding on the part of everyone involved. Everyone pays attention to who says what, what it means, the tone of what is said, the beliefs and values of the context in which something is said, and the meaning for all levels of the context—for example, the individuals, the groups, and the community as a whole. Everyone involved in this process thus becomes aware of the collective thinking, learning, and understanding. With this collective thinking, learning, and understanding, new discoveries emerge and creativity becomes part of the norm (p. 51).

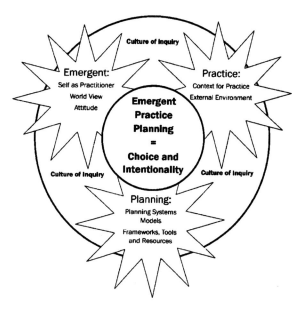

Figure 2.2. Emergent Practice Planning Framework.

In this culture of inquiry, there is a process of listening, processing, integrating, and understanding on the part of everyone involved.

3

Emergent-Self as Practitioner

Key Themes: *What I believe about change, choice and practice... What theoretical orientations guide my practice... My evolution in practice...*

Reflections: *I have been a clinical social worker for 25 years. When I look back at my work, I laugh and then cry. What took me so long to figure this out? Do I have it figured out? I suspect that today is another beginning...*

Self as Health and Social Services Practitioner

In this section, you have the opportunity to begin looking at and seeking to understand yourself as a health and social services practitioner. Health and social services work is very personal work. You take your beliefs, values, attitudes, life history, previous experiences, cherished theories—in other words, all of you—to every aspect of and setting for your practice. "Wherever you go, there you are!" (Elsdon, 1998).

It is often said that being effective in health and social services work demands that you stay personal. Actually, being personal is not quite enough in that everything we do is personal. Health and social services work actually demands that we use the self, and all that being the self connotes, to do our practice. Projecting oneself in practice does not just happen. To do so requires awareness and planning and, therefore, intentional use of the self. It is taking a deliberate course of action in light of the total context, and the context most definitely includes the practitioner.

> Projecting oneself in practice requires awareness and planning and, therefore, intentional use of the self.

The challenge is to know the self at any point in time, because not only is your practice emergent, but you are too. You are always in a state of change, so to have the capacity to project yourself into practice requires that you be able to monitor, understand, and use the emerging self. Clearly the emerging self contributes to the emergence of your practice. This section will help you decide how you can monitor and use the emergent self in practice.

Emergent Frames and Filters

As we reflected upon our own experiences with case planning, and practice in general, we realized that there is a series of filters through which people make sense of their practice. Exceptional practitioners operate within a different frame of reference from less-effective practitioners and systems.

> We believe the most effective practitioners (and systems) are open to their emergent nature and the emergent process.

Fundamentally, we believe the most effective practitioners (and systems) are open to their emergent nature and the emergent process. Some of the shifts in attitude and approach that we think are important are presented in Table 3.1.

Filters	From typical	To exceptional
World view values and attitudes	Judgment: If it doesn't work, it is my fault, or the fault of others. Pessimism: It won't work. Control: I need to control this; I need to be in control. Simplicity: Make things simple.	Curiosity: I wonder… Optimism: There has to be a way. Complexity: Recognize and work with complexity.
Context	Fragmentation, reductionism: Isolate the concerns, narrowly focused attention, work alone.	Holistic: Work within the bigger picture with partners, focused on the larger view and multiple options.
Professional self	Separate professional self: I am defined by my profession, discipline, position, and job and act accordingly.	Integrated self: I take myself everywhere I go; professional and personal are interconnected, interrelated, and integrated.
Professional responsibility	Knowing: Be the educated expert; have the answers.	Learning: Recognize areas of expertise, knowledge, and strength and know that I don't know and that we can figure it out.
Professional accountability	Control of resources, efficiency and effectiveness: How do we get more "bang for the buck," reduce costs, and use time and resources well?	Quality of care, mindfulness of costs: I need to understand the perspective of others and then share the expertise I have in ways that work both for the individuals affected and for the systems.

Table 3.1. Shifts in Attitude and Approach

All of these shifts could be part of the personal in emergent practice. If you accept that things are complex and interconnected, that you don't know, that you need to seek out and include others in your processes, and that long-standing curiosity works better than frequent judgments, then you are probably open to continuously reflecting upon your experiences. You are also probably open to understanding yourself as a practitioner. Where would you situate yourself in this framework?

Emergent Self-Awareness

One of the challenges presented to you in this book is to make congruent your vision of practice and being the practitioner. It is about being an intentional practitioner. It is about being a practitioner who projects the self in practice and deliberately uses the self in practice. For example, we frequently experience people who lament that they cannot practice the way they would like to due to barriers created by the systems. However, when asked how they would like to practice, they often find it difficult to articulate what they would like to do and what prevents them from doing it.

> Being an intentional practitioner is about being a practitioner who projects the self in practice and deliberately uses the self in practice.

There is no doubt that systems can create multiple challenges and barriers to effective practice. However, if we do not know the emerging self, our purpose in practice, and how to be strategic in terms of the total context, we are unlikely to overcome the challenges and barriers confronting the client or ourselves. Further, without knowing the self we cannot make informed choices about whether to stay within a system or move on. We don't have the option to select systems that we like and choose to be a part of them.

If you are uneasy or uncomfortable with your current practice, we encourage you to examine and discover the emerging self. Use this process of inquiry and trial to see what themes arise. Examination of the emerging self, and how to use the self in practice, is a process of revisiting and discussing beliefs and values, and theoretical orientations. The separation of the personal and professional self is an artificial and useless distinction. Instead, place importance on introspective reflection as a research practitioner.

Nested Belief Systems as Practitioner

Belief systems are complex systems of thinking that organize our daily decision making and functioning. Belief systems are our representation of what is, how things work, and what we can and cannot do, and they constrain the options that we experience moment by moment. The capacity of practitioners to understand that their belief systems are compositions of worldviews, visions, beliefs and values, and purpose in practice is

> Belief systems are our representation of what is, how things work, and what we can and cannot do, and they constrain the options that we experience moment by moment.

critical to executing EPP. These aspects of belief systems are nested, or interrelated, and when shifts occur in one area, they likely occur in other areas.

Worldviews and Attitudes

Worldviews and attitudes influence how you see the world, and they inform your opinions about the world. In the world of practice there are practitioners who believe that people are basically good and that when given the healthy option, they will take it every time. Others consider people to be rational choice-making beings; they are responsible for what happens to and around them. Still others see the world as basically safe or unsafe, benevolent or bad, benign or unkind, a challenge or an opportunity, and so on. Major attitudinal points of view color everything. For example, optimism colors experiences as rosy or yellow, whereas negativity colors them as black or gray.

As practitioners we have many worldviews and attitudes, some of which are unknown to us. One way to become aware of your worldviews and attitudes is to pay attention to the often-repeated injunctions that appear in your thinking. Injunctions are those authoritative admonitions, warnings, or orders that you put out frequently and across situations. They are often in the form of meta- or overriding, rules and they represent fundamental beliefs about how the world is or should be. Examples of worldviews and attitudes in practice include:

- It's all about power and abuse of power.
- Change the attitude to change the behavior.
- Change the behavior to change the attitude.
- You can't change what you don't know.
- What a wonderful world!
- Life is hell.
- Who cares?
- Work hard no matter what.
- No motivation, no change.
- Never mind.
- I can't do anything about this.
- There must be a better way.
- Lead, follow, or get out of the way.
- Wow, what an opportunity!
- Won't happen, forget it.
- If you want something done, do it yourself.
- This is hard but worth doing.

Embedded in these injunctions are beliefs and values about aspects of self, others, and practice. For example, the statement "You can't change what you don't know" is based on the belief that change is related to knowing and not knowing and that change is possible. But the client has to know what he or she wants changed. The statement is valuable because it implies that knowing is important, and without knowing, change is not possible. Another implied value is that change is important; otherwise, we wouldn't be talking about knowing and change. As another example, the belief embedded in the statement "There must be a better way" is that there are many ways, and some ways are better than others. Further, it is possible and desirable to find a better way. Finding better ways is important in practice (value) and therefore we say there must be a better way.

Beliefs and Values

The examples used above illustrate that our worldviews and attitudes reflect our beliefs (i.e., what we hold to be true), our values (i.e., what we hold to be important), and how we conduct ourselves (i.e., the injunctions we live by). Our experiences in life and our interpretation of them influence our belief systems. In other words, our beliefs and values come out of our interactions in the world with others. Family beliefs and values are extremely influential because we interact with family members for significant periods of time.

By understanding how our beliefs and values are reflected in our injunctions or rules, we can see how they influence our practice. Our beliefs and values are evidenced in our thoughts, feelings, and actions when we are deciding whether to work with someone, conducting an interview, writing an assessment, or deciding what to do in the moment. An example of these interconnections from the perspective of a health and social services worker who works with teen parents is presented in Table 3.2.

Note that the truths need not be universal truths. For example, you may believe that the sun rises in the west and sets in the east. If you believe strongly in this, you don't care that the empirical evidence contradicts your belief. To take a more realistic example, people who believe it does not matter what they do because nothing will work out for them will probably have difficulty experimenting with new strategies. No matter what coaching or encouragement you give them, because the belief is strongly held, it will be difficult to shift.

Use the questions in Table 3.3 and write down some of your beliefs, values, and rules that relate to your practice. Start with your beliefs. What are your beliefs about your strengths and limitations? About being a man or woman as practitioner? About being a change agent? What is your capacity and potential as practitioner? What do you believe about your current practice context? What do you believe about adjusting yourself to your practice

Beliefs: What I hold to be true.	Thoughts: My internal dialogue.
It is true that you need an education to get ahead in this world.	Jamie needs this education.
It is possible for anyone to get ahead in the world.	If she doesn't get it, she and her baby will be stuck in the welfare cycle.
One can get stuck in a welfare cycle.	
Value: What I hold to be important.	Feelings: My emotional reactions.
It is important to pursue an education, regardless of the hardship that it presents.	Frustration that Jamie is not applying herself.
It is important to get ahead in the world.	Sadness as the baby's future is anticipated.
It is important not to get stuck in the welfare cycle.	Having no control over what Jamie will do.
Rules: How I conduct myself.	Actions: What I do.
Life can be different.	Cajole Jamie into sticking with her educational program.
Get an education.	Enlist the help of others to keep her in it.
Stick with it.	Help her get application forms.

Table 3.2.   Belief Systems

Beliefs: What I hold to be true.
It is true that ...
Value: What I hold to be important.
It is important to ...
Rules: How I conduct myself.
The rules I live by are ...

Table 3.3.   Belief Systems about Practice

context? What are your beliefs about assessment, decision making, planning, and choice in practice? What do you believe about self-determination in terms of yourself as practitioner and in terms of your clients?

Next, consider your values. What values are embedded in your definition(s) of practice? What values do you refuse to compromise in practice and which ones are more negotiable? What work context values are inconsistent with your values? What aspects of your professional code get challenged within your work setting? How do you maintain professional integrity (being true to your values)? What values do you hold in terms of being a man or woman? Which of your limitations do you not value enough to work on? How important are choice, self-determination, assessment, decision making, and planning in your practice? What do you take as evidence that these aspects of practice are, or are not, important?

Now consider your rules. What rules do you have that show up in your practice? What are your rules for documentation? Assessment? Planning? Decision making? For being a man or woman practitioner? What rule(s) do you have about maintaining personal integrity? Under what conditions do you not follow your own rules? In other words, what is the metarule?

If you struggled with this exercise, do not be dismayed. This is normal and to be expected, given how little time we spend making explicit our beliefs, values, and rules for practice. Although our thoughts, feelings, and actions are manifested through our beliefs, values, and rules, we are more often aware of them than the underlying beliefs, values,

Our thoughts, feelings, and actions are influenced by the context in which they occur, and are thereby manifested by context-bound beliefs, values, and rules.

and rules. Further, our thoughts, feelings, and actions are influenced by the context in which they occur, and are thereby manifested by context-bound beliefs, values, and rules. Often, by being curious about why we have certain thoughts and feelings, or act in certain ways, we begin to identify and explore the beliefs, values, and rules that guide us. By doing so, we come to understand how they vary depending on context.

Now we encourage you to extend your inquiry about beliefs and values, first for yourself, and then for the teams, organizations, and systems within which you work. Reflect on each area of inquiry in Table 3.4 and note down your thoughts in the space provided.

It is also important to be open to exploring the beliefs, values, and rules of others, particularly those of the people we serve. Knowing the shoes we walk in, and being open to walking in another person's shoes, can go a long way towards building understanding. As examples, consider the following stories that were shared in the context of a training session on conflict resolution.

The first story begins with the words of a staff person who was seeking to control a conflict that she had with a client.

> James has been on welfare for years. He's a long-termer. He can't work anymore. The
> problem is, every time he comes into the office for some help he is unbelievably rude

and demanding. He treats everyone badly. He waves that cane of his, yells, and makes unreasonable demands. It's to the point where, when I see him coming through the door, I want to run away. I've just had to become really firm with him and tell him that if he misbehaves then he won't get what he came for. It really makes me mad, too, because he's always defending his sons and demanding things for them too. They are really messed up, but he doesn't seem to want to take any responsibility for their behavior. What can I do to stop him from creating all this conflict in my life?

This example presented us with an opportunity to understand beliefs, values, and differences and how these influenced thoughts, feelings, and actions. I asked the group to tell me more about James. What I noticed was that the description of James was often interpretive and judgmental—for example, "He is an outcast." Over time, the following information came out about James. He is a forty-something ex-logger. Ten years ago he was hurt badly in a car accident and has been unable to work in the woods since. At the time of the accident he was married to Jean and they had two young sons. They owned a home, vehicles, boat, and furnishings. The family tended to keep to themselves and rarely socialized with other members of the community. Little was known about the family. After the accident James was unable to receive any disability pension or assistance. He wasn't able to find any other

Area of Inquiry	Personal Beliefs and Values	Organizational Beliefs and Values
The nature of the systems within which I work		
The needs of the people being served		
The capacity to do the work (personal and systemic)		
Barriers to change		
Rules/policies and rule/policy compliance		
Choices and lack of choice; discretionary authority and lack of authority		
Power, control, management		
What is good and not good practice		
One right way or many good possibilities		
What are good and not good outcomes		
Ethics and ethical practice		
Conflict and disagreement		

Table 3.4.   Belief Systems for Aspects of Practice

work, probably because he had only an eighth-grade education and had few marketable skills outside of the logging industry. In time, James and Jean had to sell the house and their other assets. Jean left James six years ago and moved to another community. James and his sons now live in a run-down, two-bedroom apartment. His sons, in their mid- and late teens, have spent time in youth detention for property crimes. Neither of them is going to school. Members of this small community have been quite critical of both James and his sons.

The tone of the conversation began to shift as we tried to understand more about James. We then began to consider beliefs and values, first exploring those that the practitioner held and then speculating on those that James might hold. For example, the practitioner held the belief that "people are responsible for their circumstances and can make changes if they wish." She held a value that "it is important for people to work hard to make their lives better for themselves and their children." A related ethic or rule was "work hard and be industrious." James, on the other hand, might hold a belief that "I can do nothing to make my situation better,"; "the state owes me a living because I am disabled,"; "you have to fight to get what you need," or "the workers don't care about my family." His values might include "it is important to protect my children from criticism" or "it is important to get whatever I can out of the system for my family." Related ethics or rules might be "stick up for myself," "be demanding," or "don't take no for an answer."

Clearly, there are conflicting belief systems in place here that influence not only how each individual acts, but also how they interact. What was interesting was that the practitioner and her colleagues fell silent for a few moments after reflecting upon their own and James' belief systems. The practitioner then said, "I think I'm going to try things differently next time."

The second story begins with the words of a family member who came for family counseling. In this case the beliefs and value conflicts are within the family.

> **Wife**: I know that he is having an affair. Even though he promised 16 years ago to love and cherish me and to be faithful to me, I know that he is running around with other women and it is likely that he will leave me. It is just a matter of time. When we first married life was wonderful. We had so many things in common and he was so kind and caring. Not at all like my dad, who intimidated and bullied my mom. I will never understand why my mom stayed in that loveless marriage. Well, I won't put up with it. I will not be in a loveless marriage. Once I prove that he is having an affair I am out of here and I will take him for all he is worth, which isn't much. He's not much of a father and our fighting in front of the kids is harmful. It would be better for them if we split up.
>
> **Husband**: I remember getting married. What a horrible day that was. All my single buddies showed up after the party the night before and we looked like "h-." I knew I had lost my freedom and that it would never be the same again. "Why was I doing this?" I wondered. "I don't even have fun with her. She can't do sports or hunt or fish; she just wants to go to movies." But I think we had better stick it out for the kids; they will only be around for a few more years. Two parents are better than one. Besides, I cannot afford to support two households. My folks split up when I was a teenager and I said that I would never allow that to happen if I ever had children. It's not fair for teenagers to have to deal with being a teenager and their parents splitting up.

This example gives you an opportunity to understand different beliefs and values and how these influenced their thoughts, feelings, and actions. It also presents you with an opportunity to explore

- Your attitudes toward affairs in marriage
- Marriage and divorce
- Factors that affect marriage
- Divorce effects on children
- Timing of divorce effects on children
- Other information needed to work with this family.

Would it be desirable to work with the family members separately or together? Would you work with the couple and then the children and then the whole family? What beliefs and values would influence your decision?

Do you ever understand sufficiently the worldview and experience of the person, family, or group that you are serving to be able to project them as they are understood by the client? Perhaps—but perhaps not. Although you may not be right or never know if you were right, the commitment to seek understanding will engage you in a mutual learning process. You will be involved in a process in which curiosity wins over judgment, and interest in others wins over positions about them. It is not necessary to give up your own beliefs and values to do this, although you may choose to change some of them. You do, however, need to distinguish between your beliefs and values and those of your client and others in the practice context, as this is the only way that you can attempt to understand their circumstances and experiences. We encourage you to seek such a broader under-standing so that you can work and within the client's context.

When you use a reflective practice approach, your inquiries are more likely to include the following:

- What does the client, family, group, or community say?
- What do they say it means?
- What beliefs does the client, family, group, or community have?
- What are they holding to be important?
- What rules do they live by?
- Why these rules?
- What has influenced these rules? For example, have culture, ethnicity, experi-ences, and exposure influenced them?
- What are their hopes and their fears?
- When were their hopes dashed, and by what?
- Where do these fears originate? Are they unfounded?
- What is their capacity to deal with this? What do they say about their capacity to deal with this?
- What other resources can they access from family and community?
- Who else knows something about this situation?
- Who else can I engage?
- What do I need to understand better and know more about?
- Where do I need to go to access greater understanding or to learn something I don't know?

This type of inquiry shifts our perspective from that of knowing, to being someone with expertise, compassion, and a capacity to learn and work with others.

Vision and Purpose in Practice

Purpose and vision are related to the practitioner's intentions, deliberations, and reasons for being in practice. Practice is not a mindless adventure. It is deliberate action directed towards the practitioner's intent or purpose. You practice in order to resolve something—to answer a question, to solve a problem, to bring about change, to demonstrate virtuous conduct, such as making the world a better place. In short, you have an objective in mind. When you have a purpose, you are up to something, you are headed somewhere, you have intentions about the result and are deliberate in how you promote or prompt the result you have in mind.

Practice is not a mindless adventure. It is deliberate action directed towards the practitioner's intent or purpose.

Effective practitioners dare to dream; their visions are big.

Because practice is something you put your mind to, it involves a kind of imaginative insight, or foresight, which we call *vision*. When you are purposeful in your practice you begin to formulate a vision—likely a shared vision—of what could be, how things might be different, or how the story could have a different ending. New possibilities come to mind, get embellished, and turn into imaginative views of what can happen and how someone's life can be different. This shared vision offers hope and focus (see Figure 3.1). Effective practitioners dare to dream; their visions are big. Some purposes are listed below.

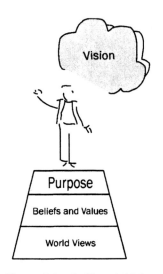

Figure 3.1. A Shared Vision Offers Hope and Focus.

- Make the world a better place to live.
- Improve the quality of life for individuals, families and communities.
- Bring about peace and harmony for all.
- Ensure equal access and participation, regardless of race, gender, ethnicity, or other diversity.
- Promote social responsibility in the world.

When you are clear about your purpose in practice, then your shared visions of client outcome will likely take on definitions related to your purpose. For example, if you are a practitioner committed to making the world a better place, your plan of action will likely promote a better world for your clients. If you focus on bringing peace and harmony to the world, then your plans will reflect what needs to change for the client to experience peace and be in harmony with the self or others. Purposes are different platforms for practice. They shape the definition of what we consider the client to need and how circumstances, or this person, might be different. It is useful to consider whether the practitioner's purpose can be set aside when the client's purpose is incongruent. Often in the early stages of working with clients, they ask about the focus of your practice. Do you suggest they go elsewhere if there is a perceived difference about the purpose of working together? What do you do when there is nowhere else for them to go?

Theoretical Orientations

Our theoretical frameworks establish another filter or lens through which we orient our practice. These frameworks also reflect purpose and vision. Perhaps there was a time when people embraced one particular theoretical framework, such as behavior therapy or psychoanalysis, and defined themselves and their practice by that standard. Today, it is rare to find practitioners who live and practice within just one theoretical orientation; more often, people practice in ways that suggest the influence of a number of different but compatible theoretical frameworks.

Behavior change theoretical orientations are used in practice to explain how people become who they are, and from that, how to help them change. These orientations have their respective views of behavior and levels of behavior; for example, individual versus family versus community behavior. As such, they bring focus to different aspects of behavior in terms of deciding what to assess, what the problem is, and what to change.

> Ontological beliefs and metaperspectives represent beliefs and reflect values that are deeply embedded within the practitioner's—and sometimes the organization's—philosophical position.

Often these theories are embedded in ontological positions (what they believe to be true about behavior and how to change it) or in metatheories or perspectives. Ontological beliefs and metaperspectives represent beliefs and reflect values that are deeply embedded within the practitioner's—and sometimes the organization's—philosophical position. For example, more current perspectives of feminist therapy and critical strategies suggest that social interventions should be aimed at being socially responsible, although they may not have articulated therapy strategies. Sometimes, their practice takes the form of promoting gender equity by working with an individual to free her from being oppressed or through community advocacy work. One wonders if a practitioner takes a position of promoting peace and harmony, then theoretical orientations that address issues in systems, or feelings, or conflict resolution may be more effective. Sometimes disagreements evolve in terms of what to do; will we do it your way or my way? Consider the possibility that the disagreements are less about what to do and more about different purposes and understandings of the nature of the problem. How we view, or what we consider to be true about, the nature of the problem defines what we believe can or cannot be done to change it.

Behavior-change theoretical orientations have their own frameworks and models for identifying and dealing with problems, but a lengthy discussion of them is beyond the scope of this book. Any text on clinical or theoretical orientations for behavior and behavior change would be advised for those not familiar with theoretical orientations. You might also be interested in theoretical orientations for organizational and community change, which are likely to be located in business, organizational psychology, and sociology literature. The evolution of different disciplines has resulted in a proliferation of new practitioners who bring with them new theoretical orientations.

Some theoretical orientations and their perspectives on human behavior and change are presented below. These perspectives are provided to demonstrate how the focus of practitioners varies, depending solely on their theoretical orientation. Their orientation actually dictates what behaviors would be explored as potentially "troublesome" behaviors. This initial step in exploration sets the stage for the rest of the inquiry: the formulation of needs and goals; the choice of interventions and strategies; and the indicators for determining progress towards change. Another way to think about theoretical orientations is "believing is seeing." Because believing affects what you see, how you see things affects what you end up thinking, feeling, and doing—in other words, practicing.

Psychoanalytic Theory

This is a theory of personality development, a philosophy of human nature, and a method of therapy that focuses on how unconscious factors motivate behavior. Psychoanalytic practitioners believe that the first six years of life are determinants of the later development of personality. Further, they assume that faulty personality is the lack of resolution of successive psychosexual and psychosocial stages of development. Therefore, assessment focuses on the client's early history and may use projective or other personality tests to identify themes apparent in the client's life. A formal and comprehensive assessment is required in order to understand the emotional disorders of the personality.

Adlerian Theory

This neo-Freudian therapy focuses on the client's faulty perceptions and assumptions about life that affect current functioning. It is a "growth" theory that stresses taking responsibility, creating one's own destiny, and finding meaning and goals to give life direction. The assessment is made early in therapy and involves determining one's view of self, others, and the world. Comprehensive data are collected on the family and on early recollections.

Person-Centered Theory

Developed in reaction to psychoanalytic therapy, this orientation is based on a subjective view of human experience. It places faith in, and gives responsibility to, the client in dealing with her or his problems. This therapy argues that the client knows best the dynamics of her or his behavior, and the focus of therapy is on getting the client to experience a perceptual shift in behavior. Therefore, external and objective assessments are viewed as intellectualizing about the client, thereby missing the point, which is to get the client to assess in the moment and to determine the need for a shift and how to do it. Key to working with clients is unconditional positive regard and emphasis on developing an unconditional relationship.

Behavior Theory

This theory applies the principles of learning to the resolution of specific behavioral disorders. Behaviorists seek information on present behavior in order to generate a treatment plan for the client. More specifically, the behaviorist asks questions about past learning as it relates to current behavior patterns. An objective assessment of specified behaviors and the stimuli maintaining or reinforcing them is required. Results are subjected to continual experimentation or trial. The focus of the approach is on the use and continual refinement of techniques to bring about behavior change.

Rational-Emotive Theory

The premise of this theory is that people construct faulty thinking and irrational beliefs from their experiences. Attention is paid to those events that resulted in certain beliefs and to changing the undermining, self-defeating beliefs with constructive ones. The focus in assessment and therapy is on patterns of thinking, recognizing that the client has constructed these patterns from her or his experiences.

Reality Theory

This short-term therapeutic approach focuses on the present and stresses the client's strengths. Using a prescriptive process, clients learn more realistic behaviors to achieve success in their lives. Assessment is not formal since the focus of therapy is to get clients to critically examine what they are doing now and determine to what extent it is working for them. The informal assessment focuses clients on their successes, strengths, and assets in the moment. The intervention focuses on keeping clients aware of their reality and how they make the planned change. If the change is not made, clients are confronted with the responsibility of either sticking to their plan or making up a new plan that they can get to work. This approach emphasizes the client's choice, and the responsibility that comes with choice.

Systems Theory

The focus of family systems assessment and intervention is on the structure, dynamics, and communication patterns of the system. Basically, systems therapists argue that families have created or organized their lives and that their organization is represented in the structure or patterns of interactions. Families must first understand how they operate (their patterns of interaction) and what benefits they derive from behaving the way they do. Only by understanding this can families decide what and how to change. Since systems therapists know that systems are always changing, assessment is ongoing and viewed as a part of intervention.

Critical Theory

Critical theorists believe that reality cannot be objectively understood since reality is shaped by social, cultural, political, and gender-based values that shift over time. The aim of critical theorists is to expose and make transparent the value sets that underlie reality and expose it for what it is, a social construction. They critique the institutions and systems that maintain the dominant (e.g., "patriarchal," "capitalist," or "industrial") views of reality and advocate that these systems and institutions be reformed or overthrown. Personal and social problems are viewed as embedded in the system rather than in individuals. Critical theorists draw on different techniques and strategies in practice but emphasize experiential knowing and encourage reflection. They encourage reflection to assist people in gaining an understanding of their circumstances and oppression.

Feminist Theory

As a branch of critical theory, feminist theory holds that reality (and theory) has been defined largely by white males and that women's experience has been discounted such that women have become alienated from themselves. The presumption that there is "one reality," or indeed any reality, has been challenged by feminists and feminist theorists who critique the dominant and oppressive systems and institutions as well as the beliefs that are held in society about women, relationships, and families. Feminist theory practice involves deconstructing ideologies, systems, and institutions and exploring different ways that situations can be understood. Emancipation and fundamental social change is an objective of feminist theory.

Narrative Theory

Narrative approaches focus on life stories that are captured in the details and interpretations of the events in a person's life. The practitioner focuses on understanding how the interpretations are rule-bound within a particular discourse and how they represent issues of power. It is important to access silenced stories so that the different stories can come together in a new way. Attention is paid to how the client resists having the new story come together, and the therapist works with language to reshape events into different narratives. By changing the story, one can live a different story.

Believing Is Seeing

Because "believing is seeing," it becomes apparent that the practitioner's theoretical view influences practice in a major way, from beginning to end, so to speak. Starting with the premises of the different theoretical orientations, problems are going to be related to

- Faulty premises
- Emotional blocking that affects thinking
- Ineffective learned behavior
- Faulty thinking and irrational beliefs
- Interactive sequences of behavior where one behavior influences the next
- Narratives that reveal issues of power.

The different premises affect what gets listened to, heard, and probed. Behavior-change theoretical orientations are powerful models that are used to define the nature of the problem, as well as how to address it.

Clearly these models are not mutually exclusive. We may be influenced by a number of them as we formulate our own orientation. Indeed, Corey (2001) suggests that as practitioners we should pay attention to what our clients are thinking, feeling, and doing, and in order to attend to these multiple representations of the self, we may need to draw upon and integrate several orientations.

It is interesting to consider what makes you a "brand x" practitioner. Practitioners who assess a family from a systems perspective would likely look at the structure of the family in terms of preferred transactional patterns and rules about who participates and how. If in a discussion a practitioner says, "Good idea. Let's explore that," and nods at observations that point to patterns and rules, is that practitioner using behavioral techniques? Does that make the practitioner a behaviorist? What criteria define practitioners in terms of their theoretical orientation? Is it how they think about the situation, what they do, or both? Can practitioners be eclectic? Can practitioners be integrated theorists? What is the difference? What about perspectives that offer a broader worldview and affect practice—for example, feminist, critical, or postmodern views? These broader views have values that are no doubt embedded in your practice. Do they result in an articulated theory of practice? Do they offer specific practice technologies? Do they offer a value base from which to work?

The significance of the diversity of theoretical orientations to practice is threefold:

1. *Personal influence*
   Our theoretical orientations influence how we make sense of our experience and the experiences of others. Therefore it is important to know the models that influence your practice, why you chose them, and how they apply.
2. *Interaction influence*
   The people you work with, both clients and colleagues, may have different theoretical orientations (which may be implicit or explicit). The models of practice for each will influence the information that is important to them, their perception and interpretation of events, and what they establish as desirable goals and interventions. Their models will affect you and your practice.
3. *Systemic influence*
   Professional schools, disciplines, and organizations sometimes profess to orient themselves around certain theoretical frameworks. This may influence the expectations for practice that are defined in policies and other "rules" (both formal and informal) within a particular setting or organization. When you work within or with these different policies, your own practice and theoretical frameworks may come up against those embedded in and embraced by the work setting. You may also experience pressure to adopt frameworks that you may not be entirely comfortable with because they are incongruent with your personal theoretical orientation.

To help you make your theoretical orientations more explicit in your inquiry, ask yourself the following questions:

- What theoretical orientations have I learned about, been exposed to, or been encouraged to accept? How has this influenced my beliefs about people and change?
- How do I like to work (e.g., with individuals, families, or groups; intensively, short-term, long-term)?
- What information do I seek when inquiring about the situation? From whom? How?
- What meaning and significance do I give to this information?
- What perspectives do I hold about people's capacity and responsibility for change?
- What judgment or value do I place on different theoretical orientations (e.g., do I view one as better than or more legitimate than another)?
- What is the effect of any of my judgments?
- What theoretical orientations do my colleagues seem to use and how does this influence our work together?
- What theoretical orientations do the leadership or management of my agency hold and how does this influence my work?

- What theoretical orientations do I reject out of hand, and how does my rejection of them relate to my beliefs and values?
- What new ideas are emerging out of my experiences and within my orientation?

Taking Yourself Wherever You Go

In health and social services work, we are sometimes strongly encouraged to adopt a distinct professional self. This is expressed in such statements as:

- Do not identify with your clients.
- Act in accordance with the rules of professional conduct.
- Do not seek to do your personal growth work through your work with clients.
- You are supposed to be the expert.

All of this seems sensible in the context of practice insofar as it serves to focus on the interests and needs of the people being served, rather than practitioners' personal needs. However, we believe that this demarcation between professional and personal self is a fragmentation that results in practitioners being less effective in their practice.

> To integrate the professional and personal requires an understanding of the self. It requires that you take aspects of the new knowledge related to your personal and professional experiences and see where they fit what you already know and where they don't.

It is our observation that practitioners who separate the professional from the personal are theoretically and technically very informed and proficient. They have the necessary knowledge and skills to do the work, yet are unable to project themselves in their practice. In effect, they are hiding behind their stereotypes of the professional self. They might be following the book, but the people they are serving aren't living the same text. They are playing the role of practitioner rather than being the practitioner. There is a lack of integration of what they know and who they are.

The practitioner who separates the professional and personal is not integrating and is not emerging. To integrate the professional and personal requires an understanding of the self. It requires that you take aspects of the new knowledge related to your personal and professional experiences and see where they fit what you already know and where they don't. For example, a practitioner who has an integrated understanding of systems therapy, cognitive behavior therapy, and client-centered therapy may begin to read narrative therapy. The integration of these three therapies gives focus to different aspects of clients: how they feel, what they think, and how they are in relationship to things and others. When reading narrative therapy, the idea of using stories as a way of gaining the client's perspective on these multiple aspects of the self offers a new avenue for understanding. It's new and it's not new. The practitioner works with the narrative therapy ideas until they are incorporated into her existing frameworks and models. A practitioner considering how to integrate this new therapy into practice may not adopt all aspects of the theory. For example, although the narrative approach uses stories to make the power relations explicit or transparent, a practitioner could use stories to make feelings, thoughts, and the nature of relationships explicit or transparent, and not frame them as power issues.

The idea of integration and the capacity to integrate sits well with EPP because integration and reintegration are critical aspects of being emergent. Adding knowledge and skills to existing knowledge and skills results in a top-heavy and awkward practitioner. A practitioner who emerges is taking new pieces, placing them alongside old pieces, and reconfiguring her frameworks and models. In this process, the integration of the old and the new becomes something different.

It is important to remember that you take yourself everywhere you go. All of what you have experienced and learned, value and believe comes with you into the room or streetscape where you practice. Have you experienced moments when the story being told by your client resonates so profoundly with your own story that you are emotionally affected by it and it no longer makes sense to stay protected behind the professional persona? Have you experienced times when what you felt compelled to do, therapeutically, was way out of the box that you are expected to work within, but nonetheless seemed like the right thing to do? What do you do with these moments? How do you integrate them into your experience and subsequent practice? We suggest that you be willing to learn, to stay open to new ideas and experiences, and to reflect on those experiences that make you uncomfortable in order to understand the discomfort. To do this well, you must undertake to know yourself, to change yourself, and to be affected by the work you do. In other words, you must be willing to emerge.

Research Practitioner as Reflective Practitioner

A key factor in being an emergent practitioner is adopting a research-reflective practitioner stance. Being a research-practitioner is not a new idea and was originally conceived as a scientist-practitioner model (Howard, 1986; Leong & Zacher, 1991; Staatts, 1993; Tinsley, Boone & Shim-Li, 1993). The fundamental belief of research-practitioners is that information-based decision making is more valid and reliable for decision making and planning. Research-practitioners embrace inquiry and are curious to know what is going on and what things really mean. To gain understanding they ask many questions, monitor the responses, send up trial balloons, and use information from the trials to determine the next step, or to generate a plan. The practitioner is expected to perform the functions of research and practice, adapting investigative and interview skills to collect data within the context of practice and using practice-based information for clinical or practice-based research purposes.

> Research-practitioners embrace inquiry and are curious to know what is going on and what things really mean.

In the original research-practitioner concept, research was defined in terms of being scientific and was conducted by researchers or scientists. The scientific test was based on the view that there is an objective reality that could be known and was defined in terms of meeting the requirements for objective and validated information. This test included scientific methods of random assignment, pre- and post-standardized testing, and control groups. Clearly, however, and unfortunately, this perspective with its prescribed technology also separated the researcher from the research subject in order to establish objective knowledge and one separate truth (Bateson, 1972). As Rogers (1955) noted, slavish adherence to these perceptions forced us to make the unfortunate choice between "persons and science." It also forced us to decide whether we would be researchers or practitioners.

By being research-practitioners, this choice need not be made. In reflective practice (Schon, 1983; Van Gyn, 1996) the practitioner engages in an ongoing process of challenging assumptions in order to make and own choices in practice. Both the research-practitioner model and the reflective-practice model dismiss the idea that the science model offers a complete understanding of human action in the world. A commonsense understanding of our world, an inclusion of a critical approach (value-based approach), and empirically-grounded scientific studies all contribute to an understanding of human action. Therefore, all approaches to gathering knowledge are required to achieve an integrated knowledge of what is. What it comes down to is a "live and let live" acknowledgment that advocates for a broader approach to science, one that embraces the idea that information collected for clinical or practice-based decision-making and planning constitutes a way of knowing.

Information about clients, carefully collected and documented, contributes to an understanding of human beings and the world in which they live. There is no need to value one kind of information over another, and the skills for practice are in fact required in the research and vice versa. Rather than separating rationality from causality, we can develop and create different information strategies by integrating practice with scientific inquiry. New ways of thinking and new avenues for learning can only result in greater understanding and knowledge in practice.

> In the simplest terms, both research-practitioners and reflective-practitioners use their curiosity about a practice situation to stay in a state of inquiry.

In the simplest terms, both research-practitioners and reflective-practitioners use their curiosity about a practice situation to stay in a state of inquiry. In essence, inquiry is to come from a place of "knowing that you do not know," while at the same time knowing that the unknown can be known through careful probing and sensitive listening. Reflective- or research-practitioners reflect on information, generate and test solutions, and ultimately integrate what was learned into their personal practice knowledge base.

The skills of inquiry are thinking skills that involve at least four rational ways of thinking (Ricks & Griffin, 1996):

- Divergent thinking (thinking of different explanations for the same data base)
- Analytical thinking (pulling things apart to understand how the parts are related and make up the whole)
- Critical thinking (challenging underlying assumptions and premises)
- Integrative thinking (restructuring information and relating to it in order to come to a new understanding)

In this state of inquiry, using rational-thinking skills, practitioners engage in a critical function of being research-reflective practitioners—the ongoing collection and use of information for decision making and problem solving. In thinking and using information, research-reflective practitioners stay in inquiry (what do I want to know?), while asking: What will I take as evidence? What information will be useful to me and where will I find it?

Research-reflective practitioners also engage in other kinds of thinking. For example, we have talked about creative or imaginative thinking in terms of vision. Creative and imaginative thinking happens when a practitioner comes up with a crazy and far-out idea of what to do. Questioning and speculative thinking is another kind of thinking: What if? How about? I wonder about ... ? Some practitioners engage in a tuning-in process that goes beyond conventional thinking. For example, there is the intuitive hunch. It may be that when you pursue the intuitive hunch you are in an altered state of inquiry.

Some research-reflective practitioners prefer to use a scientific approach and will want to find out whether experimental studies have been conducted and whether any conclusions have been reached. In some cases a quick review of the literature (in the library or on the Internet) might meet their needs. Others will want to do a study of their own. Still others will want to speak to other practitioners about what they think and will spend considerable time with the client, carefully probing and listening.

From this inquiry and collection of information, research-reflective practitioners generate and formulate a vision and plan that can be mutually determined with, or presented to, the client. When generating solutions or alternatives, research-reflective practitioners pose each alternative as a "trial," wondering which of the strategies would work best to realize the shared vision. The trial is then put to the test through the implementation of the selected strategies. Research-reflective practitioners continue to stay in inquiry by wondering: What do I want to know about this strategy? What would I take as evidence? Where will I monitor the information?

Looking at EPP in this way, the distinction between research and practice becomes artificial and falls away. When you engage in practice from a research-reflective practitioner point of view, ipso facto, you are conducting research; when you conduct research in the context of practice, it represents a kind of practice. To invoke a broader scientific process of thinking—critical, creative, and intuitive—and trial testing throughout practice, practitioners must not only make explicit their decision-making strategies, their values and preferences, and the shared vision in goal statements, but also evaluate the effectiveness of what they do. It allows for, indeed demands, a professional accountability. In fact, professional accountability is built into the process and informs practitioners and clients. Practitioners and clients cannot escape from what they come to know and understand, and knowing and understanding comes through inquiry and trial.

Discretionary Authority and Judgments

Discretionary authority is a critical aspect of practice and another consideration for the emergent practitioner. Because every step in practice is a choice point for the practitioner and client, discretionary authority is involved at every step of the way. Authority is the power or right to

> Discretionary authority involves deciding as you see fit whether to assert your authority.

enforce obedience, or the power or right to influence or press an opinion. With these rights, however, come certain responsibilities and these responsibilities are spelled out to some extent by using the word "discretionary." Discretionary authority involves deciding as you see fit whether to assert your authority.

The challenge, of course, is knowing under what circumstances, and why, you would or would not explicitly exercise discretionary authority. Practice is a minefield of discretionary authority opportunities. Interestingly enough, many practitioners think they have no discretionary authority and claim simply to be enforcing policy and procedures. This kind of practitioner views every authority situation as one that is covered in the policy manual and therefore outside of their control or influence. In fact, they are deciding to use policy and procedures as they see fit, which is the application of discretionary authority and no doubt goes back to their beliefs about policies and procedures. Other practitioners think they are not exercising discretionary authority by wanting to be with, but not influence, the client. This kind of practitioner argues that the job is to share the moment and create the safety required for the client to change. Theoretically speaking, it is all up to the client. However, discretionary authority is always present, and the practitioner always makes judgments that apparently represent "the best fit" given the options. Discretionary decisions are choices that precede your response (see Figure 1.1). As illustrated in Figure 3.2, if it were not for choice we would simply be responding to stimuli. Your response is not a choice unless you were aware of the alternatives and deliberately chose one of the options.

Response Without Choice...

Stimulus   Response

Response With Choice...

Alternative Response

Stimulus   Alternative Response

Response

My choice!

Figure 3.2.   Stimuli-Response Versus Stimuli-Choice-Response.

> Discretionary authority comes down to deciding, to making a choice, and this requires the practitioner to know what fits and what does not fit in a case. Discretionary authority judgments will vary depending on the practitioner and the circumstances.

If you consider policies and procedures to be the laws covered in the rule book (policy manual), you are exercising your discretionary authority by going with the law. Your supervisor or fellow practitioners, on the other hand, may have a different view of policy and procedures; they may consider them to be a general plan of action that applies to most of the people most of the time. However, it up to the practitioner to decide as she sees fit whether the general plan of action is appropriate in any particular case. Discretionary authority comes down to deciding, to making a choice, and this requires the practitioner to know what fits and what does not fit in a case. Discretionary authority judgments will vary depending on the practitioner and the circumstances.

In asserting discretionary authority, we return to the need to understand the Self as Practitioner. It requires knowing one's worldview, purpose, beliefs and values, and vision, while recognizing that they are always emerging. Even so, the practitioner must be prepared to consider what is deemed to be fit today and know how it relates to the emergent self at a point in time. Although the practitioner may not have a position on everything at a point in time, the expectation is that the practitioner is able to identify when that is true and when it is not. This requires ongoing reflection on the self, owning up to what you will or will not decide, and understanding that not deciding is also a choice. It is difficult because you feel bad and you may not know why. Sometimes you know the right or best thing to do, but cannot do it; at these times, you may need to assert what you think is best, and document that the best option was not viable in light of systemic barriers or limitations. If you cannot do what you see as fit, you can at least keep your integrity by articulating what is true!

Summary

Determining how you want to be as a practitioner is no small task. To keep up with the emerging self is even more challenging. However, the benefits are impressive. Only by reflecting on yourself and your practice can you presume to be deliberate in practice. If you are anything but deliberate in practice, a good outcome is a happy accident, and a bad outcome is an unhappy accident. Accidents happen by chance, with no apparent cause. Whatever happens is unexpected and not by design.

The EPP practitioner, however, is not an accident waiting to happen. Quite the contrary, EPP practitioners are in a constant state of inquiry, wanting to learn and create a mutual plan that will unfold as expected and be in line with the vision. Most important, EPP practitioners learn from their failures.

4

Contexts and Practice

Key Themes: *The complexity of practice; characteristics of contexts; models for context.*

Reflections: *I struggle with having to keep in mind all the players and their contexts. It is so much easier to focus on the child, and maybe the family. But to keep in mind the child, the family, their different contexts, such as school, work, and community, all the different workers and their systems ... well, sometimes it is just overwhelming.*

The Complexity of Practice

Practice does not occur within a vacuum, isolated from the rest of the world. It occurs within the relationship that develops between the practitioner and the client. It also occurs in light of the multiple relationships that the practitioner and client have with the rest of the world. The practice process involves the practitioner, the client, the client's family, government agencies, community services, the community, and so on. It is this web of relationships that creates or adds to the complexity of the practice process.

> The orientation of practitioners towards the complexity of practice influences their reaction to it. A common reaction is to feel overwhelmed by complexity.

The orientation of practitioners towards the complexity of practice influences their reaction to it. A common reaction is to feel overwhelmed by complexity. To overcome being overwhelmed, practitioners tend to isolate fragments and focus their attention on what they hope will be simpler and easier to handle. This orientation to complexity results in fragmentation and reductionism and does not assist the clients. We suggest that working with the bigger picture holds more promise, however demanding that might be. In this section we explore and examine attitudes towards complexity of practice and consider characteristics of context that contribute to its complexity. These characteristics include the following:

- Settings and systems in which we practice
- Focal points and priorities for our attention (e.g., ages, presenting problems, groupings)
- Therapeutic approaches and models of care
- Collaboration and partnerships
- Resources
- Tensions and vulnerabilities in governance.

> The more we take apart the complex whole and divide it into simple and manageable chunks, the more we disconnect the pieces from their context and lose the integrity of the whole.

Finally, we propose some frameworks and models for thinking about context. These models may be useful in helping you understand how contexts operate and affect your practice.

One of the most significant shifts in our own world-view has been the realization and acceptance that life is complex. Such complexity does not lend itself to simple solutions and quick fixes. The more we take apart the complex whole and divide it into simple and manageable chunks, the more we disconnect the pieces from their context and lose the integrity of the whole. Before discussing the ways in which practitioners are challenged by complexity, we want to explore the question "How is practice more complex now than ever before?"

Conversations about Complexity

Some of the most common exchanges we hear in the halls of agencies, conference venues, and postsecondary institutions involve views about complexity. They include perspectives such as "the needs of the people we serve are more complex" or "the environments within which we practice are more complex." In most of these exchanges, complexity has a negative connotation, as illustrated in the following conversation excerpts.

One experienced practitioner to another:

Jessie: Gosh, it's nice to see you Sandy ... what's it been, about 15 years since we last met? Yeah, it was at your going-away party ... that's it! How's it going? Where are you at now?

Sandy: Nice to see you, too. I'm over at the Rainbow agency. Been there about 12 years now. I love it. Mostly do group work with youth. Where are you?

Jessie: Still with the department of misery. I've got too much invested to quit now. Only have another eight years to go and I'll be free. Wish I could say that I like what I'm doing.

Sandy: What's different for you now? You used to get really juiced with this work.

Jessie: Well, you know, you wouldn't believe it. Everything is so much more complicated and messy now. The kids and their parents are more screwed up to begin with. There aren't any resources when you need them. And the system ... well, all I can say is you were smart to get out when you did. More rules than anybody could ever remember, expectations that I couldn't meet even if I worked 24 hours a day! It's a different

world now, my friend—way more complicated. Sometimes I pine for the "good old days." Things were a lot simpler then.
Sandy: Yeah, I know what you mean. There's just so much more to think of now. It's a lot harder.

Two new recruits at an orientation session:

Alana: What do you think of the training session?
Jackie: It's OK, I guess. I was hoping that they'd be a lot clearer about what they expect. This is really tough work and the trainers just seem to be out of touch with the reality out there. Maybe they've been away from the front lines too long. I mean, they don't seem to get that things are crazy out there. It's a whole different ball game now than when they started.
Alana: I feel the same way. I'd like to know what they'd do if they had some of these cases from hell that I keep hearing about. I want to do this work, but I am anxious about being able to cut it. It's kind of like you are all alone out there.

Complexity Belief Systems

The exchanges above illustrate some of the beliefs that people hold about complexity, such as:

- Things were simple before.
- It's complicated (terrible) everywhere, but it is particularly bad where I work.
- They (other practitioners, disciplines, agencies, government departments) have it easier than we do.
- It's worse now than it has ever been!
- The complexity is the problem.
- It's too complicated, complex, crazy—we can't do anything because it is too big.
- Most people don't understand how bad (complex) it is.

These belief systems set up an attitude and a reaction to complexity that can result in the need to take action. This might include some or all of the following:

- Reducing the complexity down to manageable pieces.
- Separating the pieces.
- Putting the pieces together in a certain way.
- Only being responsible for certain pieces and not getting involved with those outside my jurisdiction.
- Looking for and following the rules to deal with my piece of the problem.
- Making it as simple as possible.

Complexity: Myth or Reality?

A great deal of time and energy is spent lamenting the complexity of practice. Is it really more complex? On the face of it, things do seem to be more complex. In most jurisdictions there are increasing numbers of people who face significant barriers and challenges to personal well-being, including poverty, family dysfunction, mental illness, addictions, poor health, history of abuse, and abandonment. The number of children and youth in crisis and taken into care is increasing; they require basic care and ongoing support for daily living. External scrutiny and criticism of practice have increased. Certainly, the nature of the challenges seems more serious. For example, in earlier times teachers reported truancy and poor attention span as their primary concerns. In more current times their responses include violence and family dysfunction.

We believe there has been a shift in public awareness that influences these perceptions of complexity. Because of advances in communication technologies and travel, we have more information about more aspects of our environments and the people in them. Therefore, we are more aware of the interconnectedness of aspects of our environments than ever before, and, as a result, are thinking in a more ecological and systemic way. This is good news in the long run as it gives us both the larger view and an overview of the interconnected and interdependent parts. However, many of us are in the midst of determining what to do with this awareness and have not yet integrated it into our way of being in the world. We want to make it easier!

If you were to act in accordance with your growing understanding about and acceptance of the complexity of life, what might you do differently? To make this question more practical, think about the scenario below and then ask yourself the following questions:

- What else would I want to know in order to understand the family's situation?
- With whom would I want to talk in order to learn more about the family?

> James and Lily and their two children have been referred to you, a family counselor. The children, ages six and eight, have had difficulties at school, and the school staff have raised a number of concerns with your agency. The school has told James and Lily that both children will need to be placed in another school if the problems persist. James and Lily reluctantly agreed to meet with you, although they indicated there may not be much point as they were thinking of moving out of the district. In fact, it seems that the family has moved a lot. The children have been enrolled in four different schools in the past two years.

Making the Shift from Simplicity to Complexity

> To simplify is to make issues easy in order to understand them and do something about them.

No doubt you discovered that you needed more information than the scenario provided, and began to suspect that there is more to this situation than the two children's behavioral problems in school. Before going any further, consider making the shift from simplicity to complexity in order to address the issues in this case. Begin by considering the difference between simplicity and complexity.

Matters are simple when they consist of just one or two parts. To simplify is to make issues easy in order to understand them and to do something about them. In health and social services practice, then, issues are going to be simple when they only involve one aspect of the case and are easy to understand. However, as will be demonstrated in the case of James' and Lily's family, health and social services practice is anything but simple. Let's return to the story of James, Lily and their children:

> As you learn more about the family and their situation you note that they have been on welfare since James lost his laboring job after hurting his back. Both James and Lily have a 10th grade education and few marketable job skills. They are both in their mid-20's, having become parents at the ages of 18 and 16 respectively. They are both estranged from their extended families and have few supportive friends. Several extended family members have contacted child welfare authorities with concerns about neglect of the children. The complaints were not substantiated but the rift between family members grew and James and Lily moved further away. James and Lily seem concerned about their children's behaviors in school but seem lost when you suggest various parenting strategies. Lily seems to be particularly upset by the difficulties, but acknowledges that she is feeling less and less able to manage the boys' behaviors at home and elsewhere. James' and Lily's response to conflicts in the past seems to have been to "run away." For example, when there has been conflict for James at work he has quit, when they have had conflicts with landlords they have moved to another neighborhood or town, and when they have had conflicts with their children's schools they have moved the boys to a different school. They both seem to believe that their situation will "get better soon" but they have few realistic plans to make it so.

As can be appreciated with this example, James' and Lily's family context includes issues related to poverty, unemployment, education, health, social and emotional development, parenting, and family supports. They are already known to or are involved with multiple systems: school, welfare, health care, and child welfare systems to name but a few.

If you were to continue to gather information, you would learn that the different parties all have a unique perspective on the issues, strengths, and needs of the family members. These perspectives are influenced by each parties' own context (including beliefs, values, theoretical orientation, job role and mandate, personal capacity, etc.) For example, the school principal and teachers are concerned about the children's behavior and academic attainment; they have a "zero tolerance" policy for aggressive behavior and won't hesitate to suspend students who violate this policy. The welfare worker is concerned about James' and Lily's employability; she expects both parents to be actively seeking work and is frustrated by Lily's reluctance to enter the workforce. James is concerned about his back injury and finding work. Lily believes that it is better for the family if she stays at home and is fearful of looking for work. The children are becoming more aware of their family's low-income situation and are feeling ashamed of being "poor" within a school that has children who come from middle-income families. This web of interconnected contexts can be quite sticky and confusing, but for this family this complexity is their reality. It is important to note that, despite the involvement of many different people in the family's life and the multiplicity of perspectives held, no one seems to carry, reflect, or even care about the "big picture" of James' and Lily's family life. The principal and teachers care about the children's behavior, but not the parents' employment situation; the welfare worker is concerned about their employment and income status, but not their children's school performance. You might argue that it is simply too much to understand the "big picture," especially when your mandate, jurisdiction, or expertise won't allow you to do anything about most of the issues and interests of a family such as this one. However, we are not suggesting that you address the range of interests alone. We are suggesting that you cannot be effective in your practice without being mindful of such complexity and the interconnectedness of issues and people within a client's life. We are also suggesting that you will likely be more helpful to your clients if you work collaboratively with the client and the other people and agencies involved in the client's life. This will be discussed in greater detail in a subsequent section.

Practice is complex because cases and programs are often entangled states of affairs involving many aspects of people's lives. As can be seen in the example above, the daily lives of clients referred for programs and services involve conditions or circumstances such as employment, poverty, educational, health, social, and emotional issues. The whole of the person or persons involved includes all of these aspects of self.

Distinctions have been made in order to allocate resources to address particular problems related to singular aspects of the self. The needs of the singular aspects of the self are designated to different government departments or authorities—for example, health, education, welfare, social services, corrections, community development, and economic development programs. As a result, clients have to go many places to access different services, and practitioners have to struggle to focus on the one aspect over which they have jurisdiction.

To deal with the reality of people's lives, it is necessary to be aware of many aspects of their lives. The challenge is to develop awareness of the complexity, and assess what we and others might be able to do while not losing sight of the interconnected nature of actions and reactions. In doing so we must also recognize and reconcile what is and what is not possible. Sometimes, even when we appreciate and embrace the complexity, and move beyond simple solutions, a situation is so complex that no amount of goodwill or resources will resolve it.

> A family was being cared for by a schizophrenic mother. The family, including a jailed father, three young boys, and a girl who was taken into custody because of familial abuse, was being re-evaluated to determine whether the girl could return home. The youngest boy, age two, was without language, the other two boys were taking care of themselves, there was no food in the house, and the house was a filthy mess and in disrepair. Mother was waiting for father to return from jail to take care of things.

This scenario is the kind of complexity encountered on a daily basis by many health and social service practitioners. In this case there are issues of psychiatric illness, violence, neglect, poverty, and long-standing trouble with the law. Simple solutions such as taking one child out of the house for a period of time will not make any difference to the overall functioning of the family. The family capacity is low. Access to resources for different aspects of the case are in different locations and under different jurisdictions. Within singular agencies with singular jurisdictions, solutions are too simple given the issues that need to be addressed in this kind of case.

> We urge you to consider the possibility that some cases are in fact complex and that you do not know what to do.

Many cases are complex, but we often treat them as if they were simple. Many practitioners worry that there is something wrong with them if they think a case is hard and don't know what to do, and they fault themselves for not knowing. We urge you to consider the possibility that some cases are in fact complex and that you do not know what to do.

Consider the possibility that you and others will do the best you can and choose the best option when it is time. Consider shifting from simple to complex in your thinking and give yourself permission to know that you don't know. Document your real assessment of what is needed and explain why you have made this particular choice or taken this particular course of action, recognizing that in some cases it will not be enough.

Complexity in Context

Case complexity cannot be separated from the environment and needs to be understood in terms of the contextual influences. It is important to consider the characteristics of the context and the way in which it influences and makes a difference in how you consider and plan options in practice.

Settings and Systems

We practice in a wide range of settings and systems. Settings include people's homes or workplaces; community environments, such as recreation and community centers; institutions, such as hospitals and jails; residential care or treatment facilities, such as group homes and detoxification centers; or private offices and agencies. Systems include governmental systems (at local, state or provincial, and federal levels), contracted systems where services are purchased by government or funded by other large entities, and private enterprises where a person or an insurer directly purchases the services or resources required. These settings and systems may be directed by legislation and regulations, and most definitely will be guided by policies and rules created for or by the setting or larger system.

One characteristic of health and social services is the shifting definition of some settings and systems as "good" and others as "bad." Public or social acceptance of these different systems comes and goes with changes in social attitudes and knowledge. For example, institutional care for people with developmental, physical, or mental disabilities was widely thought to be "good" up to 20 years ago. Nations such as the United States and Canada were applauded for creating institutions to care for people who had difficulty functioning in mainstream environments and for relieving families of the burden of care. Later, such institutional care settings and systems were condemned and many were systematically dismantled and replaced with community-based, small-group-care living environments or community outreach services. More recently, many of these newer settings and systems have been criticized and other alternatives are being proposed.

These organizational shifts reflect an openness to reflect upon what we are doing, why, and how effective and economically efficient we are in doing it. Through this process of inquiry, we discover better, or at least different, ways of organizing ourselves. However, the relevant issue is what happens within those settings and systems and how the context of settings and systems influences the practice.

We have observed settings that are wonderful and leading edge while noting that the practice continues to be ineffective and unresponsive to the needs and interests of clients. In these situations there appears to be a disconnect between the potential of the setting context and the practice that takes place within it. Conversely, we have seen practice that is exemplary within settings and systems that are definitely not exemplary. In speaking with practitioners in the latter types of situations, we are struck by their understanding of the limitations of the settings and systems within which they practice, and their capacity to bring other contextual elements to the forefront in support of good practice.

We notice that health and social services professionals speak about working in one specific setting or system; for example, "I work in a remand center for juvenile offenders," or "I work in the health care system." This is interesting because although it situates practitioners for the benefit of others to better understand where they work and what they do, it does not begin to reflect the diversity of relationships of care within the work. The place of work also fails to reflect the relationships among settings and systems that need to be taken into account in order to address the complexity of the larger context. By situating ourselves firmly within a particular setting or system, we tell only a part of the context story. We must remember that we are actually connected to multiple settings and systems, while primarily operating within one or two. For example, saying, "I work with juvenile offenders in a detention center," tells a bit of a story about who and where you work, but does not account for the diversity of young people labeled as juvenile offenders and does not hint at the interconnections between other aspects of the justice and community care settings and systems. At a minimum, the detention center setting is interconnected with the settings of policing, remand centers, courts, halfway houses, treatment centers, and community programs. The youth justice system is likely interconnected with the criminal justice, child welfare, health care, and welfare systems.

To make the settings and systems within which you work and interact more explicit in your inquiry, ask yourself the following questions:

- What are the settings and systems within which I work?
- What other settings and systems have an impact on my work and on the people I serve?
- How do these various settings and systems interact (or not interact)?
- What judgment or value do I place on each of these settings or systems?
- What effect do these judgments have on my practice and my interactions with others?

Focal Points and Priorities

> Practice contexts are also influenced by prescribed focal points and priorities, which are usually politically driven.

Practice contexts are also influenced by prescribed focal points and priorities. Cases and programs are not only sorted into settings and systems, but are also organized in terms of client characteristics such as age, presenting problems, diagnosis, or constellation of participants (e.g., family, couple, class, etc.). As with settings and systems, we have observed shifts in orientation over time, with some foci accorded higher priority than others because they are seen as more or less favorable than others.

For example, while practice with individuals has long been the norm, over time, work with family systems was seen to be more effective (including cost effective) and grew in popularity and preference. Work with community has also gained and lost favor over time. Shifts have occurred away from allocations of services and resources based upon diagnosis, towards allocations based upon functional assessment of capacity and need. Increasingly, we are seeing systems focus their attention upon early intervention, with higher priority given to early identification and intervention for children in their first five years of life. These trends come and go, influenced by such factors as current research, values and beliefs, the orientation of decision makers, and politics.

Our intention is not to engage in the debate about foci and priorities, but rather to encourage your consideration of them in light of offering practice within different contexts. Engaging in the separation of groups, foci, and priorities, without appreciating the interconnection among these elements, is risky. For example, can you attend to the needs of preschool-age children without considering the interests, needs, and capacities of their families and communities? The success of a school readiness program that helps preschoolers to develop basic numeracy, literacy, and social skills before school entry is not just about the child, but also about the child's family and community. You could create a phenomenal child-focused program and still be unsuccessful if the capacity and needs of the parents and caregivers are neglected. Is the parent able to get the child to the program consistently and follow through with activities? What support do they need to be able to do this? What is the attitude of the family and community towards schooling and learning? What can be done to promote healthy attitudes about education?

To make the foci and priorities with which you work and interact more explicit in your inquiry, ask yourself these questions:

- Who are my clients? How do the definitions of the population I serve (e.g., people with learning disabilities, children with FAS/FAE, people with HIV/AIDS, juvenile offenders, families with children in care, women in poverty, the Dock community, people with mental illness, etc.), affect my perspective about them? How does it affect the priorities in my work and the opportunities for them and for me?
- Who are my stakeholders (groups and individuals who have an interest in the operations and outcomes of your organization)?
- Who are my partners?
- What services and resources are needed and desired? Who defines these?
- In my health or social service system, what are the current preferred foci and priorities? How do these preferences play out (e.g., new program funding, reallocation of resources, media profile, diminished interest in other populations, etc.)?
- What judgment or values do I place on different foci and priorities?
- What is the effect of any of my judgments or values?

Therapeutic Approaches and Models of Care

Therapeutic approaches and models of care refer to the ways in which services and resources are organized and delivered to the people defined as being in need of them. Examples of therapeutic approaches include narrative therapy, family systems therapy, and healing circles. Examples of models of care include foster care, restorative justice, community outreach, residential treatment, and integration (i.e., inclusion of children with disabilities in regular classroom settings). A number of factors may influence the therapeutic approaches or models of care that we practice, including:

- Theoretical orientations of self, organization, and systems
- Needs, concerns, and interests of the people being served

- Experience and attitudes of the leadership and management responsible for services and programs
- Our own experiences and attitudes towards care and the provision of services
- Organizational mandate and authority (including whether services are voluntary/nonstatutory or nonvoluntary/statutory)
- Professional or public expectations
- Research findings on what is effective or not effective
- Availability and accessibility of fiscal and human resources.

As with settings, systems, foci, and priorities, a considerable amount of energy is expended within our systems assessing and debating the relative merits and failings of one therapeutic approach or model of care compared to another. There are, for example, debates going on within the justice system about the role of restorative justice, within the child welfare system about the role of family preservation, within the mental health system about secure care and involuntary treatment, within the health care system about harm reduction, and so on. Over the years, different therapeutic approaches are deemed to be "right" while others are "wrong" at points in time or within certain circles and cultures. As with theoretical orientations, the effect of the diversity of therapeutic approaches and models of care is threefold: personal, interactive, and systemic.

However, as noted earlier, our intention is to encourage consciousness about the therapeutic approaches that are practiced in order to notice any discrepancies or inconsistencies between therapeutic approaches and models of care. To assist yourself in rethinking your therapeutic approaches and models of care and to be more explicit in your inquiry, ask yourself these questions:

- What therapeutic approaches and models of care have I been exposed to, learned about, and/or been encouraged to accept? How has this influenced me?
- How would I describe the therapeutic approaches that I use?
- How would I describe the models of care that I work with?
- Is there congruence between how I intend to act and how I do act?
- What judgment or value do I place on different therapeutic approaches and models of care (e.g., do I view one as better than or more legitimate than another)?
- What is the effect of any of my judgments or values?
- What therapeutic approaches and models of care do my colleagues use and how does this influence our work together?
- What therapeutic approaches and models of care does the leadership/management of my agency value and how does this influence my work?
- What are some emerging trends in therapeutic approaches and models of care?

Collaboration and Partnerships

> Another dimension of context to consider is who else is involved and how do they work together?

Another dimension of context to consider is who else is involved and how do they work together or not work together? We refer to this as interagency or "turf" complexity. As noted earlier, many of the people we serve have complex needs that cut across a number of agency mandates and areas of jurisdiction or expertise. The people we serve may be involved with many different people, agencies, and organizations. Sometimes this multiplicity serves the client well as representatives from different agencies find ways to collaborate in support of the client. However, often this is not the case; at best there is confusion and at worst there is conflict. To illustrate this notion of interagency complexity, think of the possible connections of the following family.

> Adele is a 38-year-old Aboriginal woman living off-reservation. She is a single parent of three children, ages three, seven, and 13. Adele was diagnosed with multiple sclerosis three years ago. Although the disease is progressing slowly, she has good and bad weeks. On the good days, she capably addresses the needs of her three children; on the bad days, she needs assistance with the acts of daily living. During one particularly bad week, she was unable to care for the children and the 13-year-old stayed home from school to care for her mother and the other two children. The school raised concerns with the child welfare authorities and Adele now has a social worker assigned to monitor her parenting. Adele is on a waitlist for increased homemaker hours. Adele's three-year-old son has a cognitive impairment and receives support services at the child development center, including speech-language pathology and occupational therapy. Adele is on welfare and is challenged by living in poverty. For example, the home that she can afford is situated in a rough neighborhood and the quality of schooling is poor. Her 13-year-old daughter has run into some difficulties with some of the other youth and is often fearful of going to school. She has withdrawn from the family and Adele struggles to find ways to stay connected with her eldest daughter. The school counselor recently called Adele and asked that she come in to discuss her daughter's poor attendance. Another challenge associated with poverty that Adele experiences is getting her three-year-old to the child development center, which is located across town. Bus transportation is awkward, and the timing is poor given when she has to drop off her middle child at his school. She therefore has a difficult time making the therapy sessions that she is expected to bring her son to. Most recently, the child development center has told Adele that her inconsistent attendance is negatively affecting her son's development. Adele is positively connected to the local Native Friendship Center and is contemplating moving back to her home reservation in the hopes that extended family could assist her with raising the children as her health deteriorates. However, the reservation is isolated and the supports that she needs for her youngest child will be unavailable.

How many agencies and professionals do you think are involved in Adele's life? You are close to the mark if you guessed from eight to 10 agencies (e.g., welfare agency, child welfare agency, homecare agency, medical clinic, child development center, two schools, Native Friendship Center, reservation). There are also 10 to 15 professionals involved from these different agencies (e.g., financial assistance worker, child welfare worker, physician, nurse-practitioner, counselors of various types, teachers, speech-language pathologist, occupational therapist, parent-support worker, homemaker, child development center administrator, welfare administrator, Aboriginal support-services worker, Band administrator).

However, the question for us is not so much how many different agencies and people are involved. Rather, it is a question of how these different agencies and service providers collaborate or partner with each other and with the family. All too often, there is limited or no collaboration or partnership. The reasons for limited collaboration or partnership between the different agencies or practitioners include that they are unaware of the involvement or role of others, are too busy to make the connections with others, distrust or discount the role and contribution of others, are not encouraged to collaborate, or are in active conflict with other people and agencies. In many cases, there is either a subtle or overt blaming of the other players, including the client. This is expressed through statements such as:

- If only they'd give him the support he really needs, then he wouldn't feel so over-whelmed.
- Their criteria are just too rigid. Our services can't get to the root of the problem ... that's their job.
- If only she was more reasonable in her expectations. She expects the moon and I can't give it to her. She's not motivated anyway!

In Adele's service context there is minimal integration or collaboration. If it is happening anywhere, it is as a result of Adele putting the pieces together.

If collaboration and partnership is not the norm within the context for your work, then consider the following:

- What opportunities are there to collaborate and partner? How might this look?
- What would be different?
- What would it take for people to begin to collaborate or become partners in practice?

Imagine answering these questions as one of the practitioners involved with Adele's family. What opportunities are there to collaborate and partner? The most significant opportunity for partnering and collaborating is with Adele herself. She clearly has many strengths as a parent, she has created positive connections with the Native Friendship Center, she is thinking ahead about how best to provide for her children as her health deteriorates, and is weighing the pros and cons of moving to her isolated reservation community. What might a collaboration or partnership with Adele look like? There are many different models for collaborative or integrated practice and partnerships, which we will discuss in Chapter 5.

> Partnerships are relationships in which you work towards common goals, share the risks and profits, and commit to each other.

Partnerships are relationships in which you work towards common goals, share the risks and benefits, and commit to each other. Therefore, the starting place for building a partnership with Adele might be the development of common goals. Your theoretical orientation, the models of care that you embrace, and other aspects of your own context will influence how you go about doing this and what is possible, although through genuine listening and seeking to understand Adele's situation you will learn enough to begin the process.

There are also opportunities to build partnerships or collaborations with other agencies and practitioners involved with Adele's family. Again, your context will influence how you might be able to do this, but starting places include asking Adele what she is willing and able to participate in or support, making personal contact with others, convening a case conference, developing an integrated plan of action, regularly sharing information about who is doing what and who can do what, and so on.

Continuing with the questions posed earlier, what would be different, and what would it take for people to begin to collaborate or become partners in practice? Chances are that if collaboration and partnerships were achieved, Adele would feel more supported and have greater clarity about her strengths, what she can do, what she needs to do, and who can assist her. Practitioners from the range of agencies involved would also likely have greater clarity about what is going on, who is doing what, and what their contribution is. There may be a re-sorting of roles and responsibilities with some practitioners becoming more engaged and others becoming less so. Our experience has been that one of the most significant differences for practitioners who are collaborating and partnering is that they no longer feel isolated and burdened with having to figure it all out alone. This shift to collaboration and partnership takes different things within different contexts, although a common factor is trust. Trust is built through experience of being with others who are trustworthy. What this means in our own practice is that we seek to understand the perspective of others, we quell judgments, we are clear about what we can offer, we do what we say we are going to do, and we continuously reflect on and reassess what we have to offer and contribute this to the group.

To return to an earlier discussion, then, if things are so complex (as Adele's case illustrates), why do we persist in thinking and acting as if we are all alone and we can solve the problems ourselves? To make your views about collaboration and partnership more explicit in your inquiry, ask yourself these questions:

- Who do I work with and how?
- What do I think are the qualities of collaboration and partnership?
- How do I represent these qualities?
- How do I build trust; how do I demonstrate my trustworthiness?
- What opportunities for collaboration and partnership have I not pursued? Why?
- What would it take for me to pursue them?
- What would I have to change about myself to become a true partner?

Resources

Another context piece that we encourage you to examine relates to resources. Resources include the following:

- Financial resources
- Human resources
- Organizational resources (e.g., availability of support, guidance, supervision, and leadership)
- Policy resources (e.g., availability of clear and effective policies, standards, and procedures, as well as clarity about areas of discretion and support for exercising discretionary authority)
- Tools and techniques.

Recurring conversations that we experience in the health and social services field lament the lack of, or inadequacy of, resources. The lament often becomes the excuse or reason for ineffective practice. This view reflects a scarcity model that is prevalent in the health and social services field. Although limited resources unquestionably challenge practice, rather than lamenting, practitioners might better spend their time considering the following questions:

- What are the needs of the people we serve?
- What resources are available and where haven't we thought to look?
- What resources can be created together?
- How can we make the best use of available resources?
- Given what resources are available, what is the best that we can offer to those we serve?
- When resources are not available, what keeps us from saying and noting that they are not available?

The issue of context has been examined by considering some characteristics of contexts. All of these aspects of contexts are intertwined and interconnected, as depicted in Figure 4.1. The question is: Does this become a sticky web or a trampoline? Do you consider yourself to be bouncing energetically on the trampoline or to be mired in a sticky web to the point of being unable to do anything?

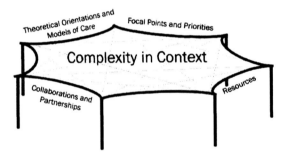

Figure 4.1. Contexts: Sticky Web or Trampoline?

Discretion allows decision makers to make the best choice from their frame of reference. But sometimes, the circumstances are so complex that no effective rule can be written.

Tensions and Vulnerabilities

We never want to lose sight of the significance of our work in peoples' lives. To label it "health and social services work" diminishes it, in our view, by distancing it from the very personal experience of relating to the individuals, families, and groups with whom we work. We are always engaged in work that has the potential to have a major impact on the lives of people. As such, it is important to recognize the unrelenting tensions among the players, which are often exacerbated by the highly emotional environment that results from the constant demand to make numerous, timely, and difficult decisions that affect the lives of others.

At times, two or more rules apply simultaneously but dictate opposing results. By using discretion, the decision makers can sometimes resolve the conflict in ways that best accommodate the interests and needs of those involved. At other times, when rules are applied to a particular case, the result will actually conflict with the intent of the rules, or will violate our understanding of justice and fairness. Again, discretion allows decision makers to make the best choice from their frame of reference. But sometimes, the circumstances are so complex that no effective rule can be written. In these cases, discretion frees decision makers to deal with the complexity, however uncomfortable it might be.

There are times when the legislation, policies, and rules are so explicit they appear to be non-negotiable. However, we can always use discretion to interpret the legislation, policies, and rules and to decide whether to apply them in the case. How do you want to exercise your discretionary authority? What will you take into account? We have come full circle back to the notion of reflection and knowing ourselves, as Garner (1998) expresses so well:

> In the day-to-day process of making discretionary choices and decisions I find myself caught up in a kaleidoscope of public opinions and institutional expectations that culminate in the demands imposed on public servants to be accountable for the expenditure of public funding. Juxtaposed to this are the critical needs of people who have very few, if any, resources, people marginalized and denied access to the privileges of those more wealthy, some who are intensely angry, some of whom are illiterate or mentally handicapped or mentally ill, some who are frightened and some who don't have a command of the language to clarify their needs (p. 4).

How do we hang onto ourselves in the face of this juxtaposition? How do we reconcile the competing interests and needs? How can we exercise our discretionary authority responsibly—and with a mindfulness of both the clients' and the systems' interests and needs?

It is not enough, in our view, to simply develop an awareness of the complex contexts within which we practice. We must also ask ourselves how we will choose to relate to this context and what we might do to shift it. These are particularly important considerations if the context within which we practice contributes to the depersonalization of the people we serve and work with, competition amongst agencies and practitioners, protection of agency and discipline "turf," belief that we must have the right answer and do it all alone, an emphasis on controlling people and situations, and a focus on simplification and fragmentation of people's life experiences rather than on the "big picture" of their complex lives. Contexts are not static. At the very least you have control over your own personal context for practice—your values, beliefs, knowledge, skills, theoretical orientations, and models of care. You likely have discretion over the ways in which you practice within the larger context. As you think about the practice context, ask how you might create a context that promotes personalization and inclusion, collaboration and partnership, mutual learning, shared power and control, and the embracing of complexity.

Context Models

When we refer to the practice context, we are referring to the ambient or surrounding conditions of practice within the larger organization or system. In addition to understanding the characteristics of larger organizations and systems, there are specific environments of particular practice situations. For example, there is a site of practice—which might be an office, the client's home, or a private setting—that is more neutrally defined. There is also the life context of the client's and the practitioner's reality that gives definition to the client's world and lifestyle, as well as to the nature of the issues being brought forward.

Fortunately in these complex times, there is more appreciation and understanding of the nature of the client's issues and how they are influenced by context. Most theories of change depend on context-based information because it fosters greater understanding of the total life circumstances and situation. Contextual information provides knowledge of

> Context frameworks are useful for considering the complexity of environments and for organizing the information about them.

people in the client's life (including the practitioner), as well as the history of the client's relationships with those people; the conditions of work, study, and religious and other cultural settings that influence and affect the client's experiences; and the significant interactions of people and these context factors in the client's life.

Because of the need to understand the client's circumstances and situation, context frameworks are useful for considering the complexity of environments and for organizing the information about them. To assist you in embracing and understanding the complexity of practice contexts, we offer three frameworks to demonstrate that context frameworks emphasize different aspects of the surrounding environment: a Self-Driven Ethical Decision-Making Model; a Social System Model; and an Ecological Model (see Appendix A).

The three models have one thing in common: all three refer in some way to fundamental beliefs, values, or cultural rules that play a significant role in the context and therefore in the situation. For the Ecological Model, the rules are represented in the macro system; in the Social System Model, the rules are represented in the controls; and in the Self-Driven Ethical Decision-Making Model, the rules are represented in the codes and in the personal beliefs and values. This suggests that the structure—the rules for who participates and how—organizes people within systems. Indeed, all three models posit that understanding the rules of the system is critical to understanding any person's issues and how these issues are related to, and influenced and maintained by, the context.

At another level, all three models are similar in that they are explicit about which aspects of the context are important. Although they select different aspects as being important, each model focuses the practitioner's attention on what needs to be considered and understood. In the Self-Driven Model the important aspects are the beliefs and values of the self relative to the beliefs and values of the codes and the situation. In the Social System model, it is important to understand how the rules impinge on the way in which the system works, and that inputs, functions, outputs, and feedback are interrelated. In the Ecological Model, some levels of the system are nested and importantly interrelated and interconnected. We suggest then that there is no single framework that captures all aspects of the context, which means practitioners need to think through what aspects of the surrounding environment they want to probe and understand better. They can then select the frameworks that are useful for their practice.

In considering models for contexts, ask yourself the following questions:

- What do I need to understand about work systems?
- What do I need to visualize about family or living contexts?
- Do I want models that describe participants and resources or models that describe how things work? Do I want both?
- When listening to a client or colleague, how do I pictorially organize their systems or contexts in my mind, if at all?
- Most models for systems and contexts are mechanistic in appearance. What other images would be useful? A growing plant or tree? Circles rather than squares?

Summary

Practice is complex because of the multiple contexts that are involved. There is the working relationship of the practitioner and client, and the relationships of the practitioner and client to their respective and multiple contexts. Different agencies and practitioners might be involved, each with their own laws, rules, policies, and procedures that may be contradictory depending on the situation. A key aspect of effective practice is recognizing the many contexts in a particular practice situation and how they affect practice.

Figure 4.2 is a compilation of the three models and points out the different aspects of context related to practice situations. We want to emphasize that no single model encompasses all the aspects and, therefore, the complexity of contexts.

> A key aspect of effective practice is recognizing the many contexts related to a particular practice situation and how they affect practice.

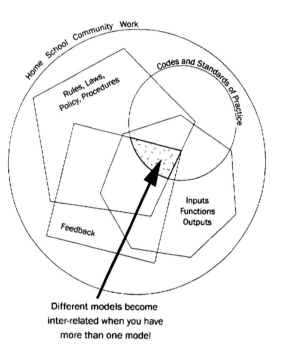

Different models become inter-related when you have more than one model

Figure 4.2.   Practice in Multiple Contexts.

5

Planning and Planning Systems

Key themes: *Planning as process; Alert, assess, and formulate case plans; Organization case planning systems.*

Reflections: *As a family counselor I just want to work with my families. Why can't I just be with these families? Why can't I just sit with them and relate to them and what they need? Why must I go through an elaborate and time-consuming process of planning and documentation? No one reads the reports anyway. No one ever checks back at the initial assessment. Why write it down? All this time could be better spent with my families. I bet I spend half my time with reports and documentation. This is a waste of time!*

Planning Distinctions: Practice Planning, Planned Change Model, Case Planning Systems

As previously discussed, emergent practitioners need to be self-aware, aware of and informed about the multiple contexts for practice, and engaged in a process of inquiry in practice. This section addresses the next piece of the EPP framework for planning. We present a framework that includes elements of a planned-change model used to formulate case plans. Each element is described and defined, and its application is discussed in some detail. Case planning systems, that is, the more explicit rules and procedures that define case management planning and practice within settings, agencies, and organizations, are also discussed.

Planning is inextricably interconnected with who we are as people and practitioners and the contexts within which we practice. Planning and practice are inseparable;

> Planning is inextricably interconnected with who we are as people and practitioners and the contexts within which we practice.

Figure 5.1.   Social Service Practices in Context.

indeed, planning is practice. As with the self and the context for practice, planning is not a discrete or one-time activity. Planning (and practice) is a continuous and never-ending process of inquiry, interpretation, and choice making. Every case is different, and every moment that we engage in the case is different. Every moment is in turn influenced by the meaning that we attribute to the moment, as well as by other choices that have preceded the moment. Faced with the exact same case two months later, or even two days later, we are convinced that the planning would be different.

There are no tried-and-true approaches that work for every case situation, no ways to standardize our planning and practice. The first part of this statement is true; the second part is not. We believe there is no way to know that a case with a certain set of characteristics should or must be addressed in a set way. Indeed, we despair at those agencies and organizations that prescribe ways of behaving and responding to certain situations and cases, using either narrowly defined and inflexible policies, procedures, standards, and other rules or house or office rules that dictate how practitioners must respond. For example, if any child (in a particular setting or program or with a particular diagnosis or problem) does "x" you must do "y"—as if all such children are the same! However, we do believe there are ways to standardize our planning and practice. These processes and approaches can assist practitioners in becoming more informed, intentional, effective, and accountable.

> Planning (and practice) is a continuous and never-ending process of inquiry, interpretation, and choice-

A Word on Language

Be advised that we use the terms "client" and "case" throughout Chapter 5. We are aware that our decision to use these terms may elicit criticism from some circles who believe that their use depersonalizes those we serve (see pp. 12–15). However, we use the term "client" to mean a "person whom we are serving" and "case" to mean a "situation," and nothing more. Thus, case in relation to practice, as in "case practice," means the action we take in consideration of individuals, groups, families, and communities and their situations. Case may refer to an individual and her or his situation or to an entire community and its situation. The planning process we present to you applies as effectively to individual cases as it does to those in which policy or program development is being considered.

We also occasionally use "case management," a term that is frequently used in practice and in the literature to refer to procedures by which situations (and clients) are considered, administered, or controlled to achieve certain effects or outcomes. Throughout most of our discussion, however, we have replaced the term "case management" with the term "case planning." This is not just a semantic shift. This shift represents movement in our own thinking and practice—from thinking about what we need to do in a technological or procedural sense with our cases so that they are managed or controlled, towards thinking more about the processes we need to engage in. Case planning systems attend to the important technological and procedural aspects of planning by specifying how people are to come together to develop plans (who, how, when, why), the elements or criteria for plans, file documentation, time frames, and criteria for tracking and monitoring progress.

> Case planning systems attend to the important technological and procedural aspects of planning by specifying how people are to come together to develop plans (who, how, when, why), the elements or criteria for plans, file documentation, time frames and criteria for tracing and monitoring progress.

The intent behind such planning processes is to understand what is going on, what we are doing with a case and why, who is responsible for what, and the effect it is having. Although this may be facilitated with assessment tools, file recording, case conferencing, and so on (to be discussed when we consider case planning systems), technology is not our starting place. Instead, it is with inquiry, and that inquiry involves engaging in a process of questioning. We make this explicit because, in our experience, even though practitioners may follow the rules and fulfill the technical requirements, it has little to do with what is really going on in the case, what is needed, what the possibilities are, and who can contribute what to address the needs. That is, it is not about inquiry.

Some Cautionary Notes

In writing this section on planning, we struggled to avoid the pitfalls that we experienced in operationalizing case management models. In our experience, planning in health and social services is seen as the procedures through which a plan will be drafted. Standards for practice routinely include statements such as "the child in care will have a plan of care that will include 'a,' 'b,' and 'c'," or "every patient file will have the following documentation." Sometimes the presence of a plan is seen as a proxy, or indicator, for being accountable. The pitfalls of such prescriptions have been noted earlier.

We have seen clients, with very different situations and needs, end up with virtually identical plans. Predictably, many front-line practitioners ignore these plans, and focus instead on the needs and interests of the client and practice. In these situations, the plan in use is different from and more relevant than the formal plan on paper.

We have also seen situations where there was either no plan or an irrelevant plan. An irrelevant plan is incomplete or outdated, fails to address the client's interests and needs (often developed independently of the client), or is unknown to or disregarded by the practitioners involved. Experienced workers sometimes defend their practice by stating that they have a plan or are following the plan, but the plan is often nothing more than a few statements about what available programs or services the client has been or will be offered. In

> Planning requires thorough assessment, reassessment, and formulation of case plans, perhaps even the reformulation of case plans.

our view, this is inadequate. Unless we know what is going on, where we are going, how we will get there, and how we will know when we do, our plan is incomplete. As you know, EPP is about being intentional in all aspects of our practice. In terms of planning, this requires thorough assessment, reassessment, and formulation of case plans, and often the reformulation of case plans.

Planning as Process

The objective of planning, be it oriented to individuals, families, groups, communities, organizations, or systems, is to bring about desired change. Plans for change don't just happen though. They need to be formulated and developed, and this requires a planning process. Most planning frameworks have components that address

- Problem identification
- Solution implementation
- Evaluation.

The framework we offer below builds on this foundation, but situates planning as a process that is context-influenced, if not context-dependent. The framework guides the planning process by helping us to focus our thinking, to make our practice more explicit, and to keep on track and be accountable. A planning framework may be embraced organizationally and a planning system may develop from it. However, the framework does not prescribe how planning should be done, nor does it define the format for the case plan. Each case plan is influenced by the characteristics and qualities of the involved practitioners, the context for practice (including the client's context), and the client's situation and needs.

> Each case plan is influenced by the characteristics and qualities of the involved practitioners, the context for practice (including the client's context), and the client's situation and needs.

As previously noted, the risk to presenting frameworks in written form is that they may be taken as linear or lock-step procedures. Although the framework below suggests there is a logical ordering or sequencing of tasks, in practice, planning is not linear. Just because a goal is set, for example, does not mean that goal setting is complete. Planning is an ongoing process, which weaves in and out and back and forth among the different elements or aspects of the planning process. The key is to have an intentional process.

The planning process framework that we propose starts with three elements:

- Alert
- Assess
- Formulate case plan.

Each of these elements, described in greater detail in Table 5.1, is multifaceted as well as context-influenced.

Planning Function	Focus of Attention
Alert	The situation, concern, issue, or problem becomes known. There may be multiple and different perspectives on what is going on. Often, referrals or requests for acting are made. Alerts are often based on pathology, although we need not stay fixed on pathology. Terms that are used for this component include case finding, identification, referral.
Assess	At the most preliminary stage, assessment is required to decide whether to accept the task of assessing the situation further, turn it down, or refer it elsewhere. Once a case is accepted, assessment, as a process, is multifaceted and includes elements of the following: 1. Clarification of responsibilities 2. Building relationships 3. Identifying information sources 4. Gathering, sifting, sorting, and integrating information 5. Interpreting information (formulating opinions, diagnoses, judgments) that identifies troublesome behaviors, underlying needs, capabilities and capacities 6. Making recommendations for a point in time. The way in which these different elements play out is influenced by whatever assessment frames, models, and procedures are in use, as well as by who is the practitioner and the client, and the context within which the assessment is being undertaken. Assessment may also be a "product" in that a report may be prepared to capture the learning and understanding about the situation that was acquired through the assessment process.

Formulate case plans	Based upon the assessment and working with those affected by the situation, a case plan is formulated using a planned change model that addresses needs, goals, service action, and evaluation, as follows. The client and other key people in the client's systems should be included in the formulation of plans.
	
	 1. Needs are identified.
	 2. Goals are set that specify the different behaviors to be in place and represent the needs identified through assessment. The goal-setting process is also multifaceted, that is,
	     • alternatives and opportunities are generated
	     • alternatives and opportunities are considered and evaluated
	     • goals are selected.
	 3. The key is that goals must have meaning to those for whom they are set (e.g., client, service providers).
	 4. Service action is specified. Service actions are the interventions and strategies that will be employed to support the attainment of the goals. The intentions for monitoring the plan and its implementation are also often identified.

Continued

Table 5.1.   Planning Functions and Focus of Attention

Planning Function	Focus of Attention
	5. Change is monitored and evaluated. Monitoring implies paying attention to what is going on with respect to the situation, the goals, the plan, and its implementation, often in accordance with some kind of criteria for observing. Evaluation is the systematic collection of information on goal indicators and/or service action. The purpose of monitoring and evaluation is to assist in assessing progress towards goals and in determining whether the goals were achieved and had the desired (or any) effect. Information obtained feeds into all of the above processes.

Table 5.1.   *Continued*

Fundamentally, this is a goal-based framework. The goal-based model poses some important assumptions for practice and practitioners:

- Practitioners can and need to function as research-practitioners. Therefore, practitioners must have the capacity to inquire, speculate, and use information in order to formulate needs, goals, and service actions and to carry out evaluations.
- Information is critical for all aspects of planning.
- Practitioners have choices in terms of interventions or strategy options, and when options are limited they must address the lack of choice.
- Data-based decision making is more informed and more likely to ensure that relevant needs and goals—with appropriate interventions or strategies—and monitoring strategies are established in the planning.
- Goal-based practice is more effective because you and your clients cannot get there if you do not know where "there" is.
- There are clear costs to clients when goal-planning for client change does not occur—that is, less change occurs.

Alert

As human beings, we are typically alerted to the need to take action when there is something troublesome in our midst or when a significant change or opportunity presents itself. Such alerts can happen in the moment or over time. For example, when a child is flushed and complaining of body aches and tiredness, this triggers someone to ask the child questions, consult a friend, or take the child's temperature and then take some action. The whole process of planning has been initiated because someone has been alerted to something that is troublesome.

> As human beings, we are typically alerted to the need to take action when there is something troublesome in our midst, or when a significant change or opportunity presents itself.

To take another example, a colleague shows you a posting for a job that seems extremely well suited to your background and interests. You have, in this instance, been alerted to a significant opportunity. You then decide whether or not to further explore it. Following are a number of examples of being alerted to something that might be troublesome.

A school counselor develops a concern about Jasper's persistent lack of attention in class and his difficulty in completing his assigned work. She may try different techniques in working with him, may share her observations with others—such as the teacher, parent, caregiver, learning-assistance teacher, child and youth care worker, or principal—or may make any number of other choices based on how she interprets and makes meaning of what is going on for Jasper. At this point her observations and concerns about Jasper serve to alert her, and any others she chooses to engage, to the possibility of troublesome behaviors. The identification of the concern is not a diagnosis (e.g., Jasper has an attention deficit disorder), nor should it be a judgment (e.g., Jasper hates school, is lazy, or lacks the necessary skills). It is simply an identification of some concern, problem, issue, or situation that may alert us to explore further.

A shift supervisor in an addictions treatment program is asked to assist one of his team members with a particular youth three days in a row and at the same time every evening. While doing so, he notes patterns that alert him to the possibility that something needs to be attended to and monitored. It may be that the team member lacks the necessary experience or skill to deal with the youth's needs, or that the youth is particularly challenging or is having an allergic reaction to something and therefore is acting out, or any number of other possibilities. The point is not to rush to diagnose and solve the problem but rather to be aware of its existence and then make a choice about whether to pursue it, and if so, how.

A community worker notes that a significant number of people who had been working the streets have not been seen for a number of days. When other street people are asked about them, they give vague or contradictory information. This situation alerts the worker to the possibility that something is amiss. Choices are then made as to whether and how to pursue the concern.

A mother talks to her minister about the family situation. She states that she is feeling depressed, misses her husband who is not around to lend a hand with their four children, and that the children are out of control. She is desperate and wonders if he knows where they can get some help.

A neighbor of a young family hears the newborn baby crying for hours each day and notes that the mom is spending time out on the front stairs without the baby, rocking herself and smoking cigarette after cigarette. This situation alerts the neighbor to the possibility that the mom is feeling overwhelmed and unable to cope, and that the child may not be adequately cared for.

Often, alerts result in referrals or proposals for further exploration. Jasper may be referred to the learning-assistance teacher for academic assessment and to the child and youth care worker for social-emotional assessment. The shift supervisor may suggest to the team member that they discuss the situation at the next team meeting so that different perspectives on the situation can be gathered. The community worker may contact the police and other service providers to propose they get together to share information on the missing street people and consider where to go next. The minister may support the mother by assisting her in going to the local community center where family counseling, youth counseling, and other services are offered. The neighbor may call the local public health nurse or the child welfare worker to raise concerns about the baby and the family.

It is important to note that alerts are often grounded in concerns, fears, or statements of pathology. While the information that alerts us to a situation may be framed in negative ways, we need not stay with a negative or pathology-based perspective on the situation. In our assessments we need to consider strengths and assets as well as challenges and deficits.

Assess

Entire books are devoted to assessment frameworks, assessment tools and techniques, and assessment criteria. Countless policies and procedures exist to guide or direct the practice of assessment, and numerous articles and chapters discuss how to conduct assessments to be consistent with one theoretical framework or another. Given this, we do not intend to tell you how to undertake an assessment. However, we do want to point out that assessment is a critical and essential aspect of practice and that you must engage in an assessment process before you undertake to set goals, define a plan, or take any other action in response to a situation.

Assessment assists us in a number of ways:

- It prepares us to undertake goal setting and planning based upon the needs and interests of the individual, family, group, community, organization, or system we are serving.
- It informs us about what is going on during and following the implementation of a service action plan, such that we can make changes as necessary.
- It prompts and assists us in documenting what is going on.

Assessment Challenges

Discussing assessment in the context of this book has challenged us for a number of reasons:

- Assessment as a process is different from assessment as a product.
- Assessment is both ongoing and discrete or defined.
- Assessment is multifaceted.
- Assessment is influenced by the context for practice.
- Assessment is something we often just do.
- There are multiple frameworks for assessment.
- Assessment demands compassion.
- We take ourselves (and all that this entails) everywhere we go.

Assessment as a Process is Different from Assessment as a Product

A great deal of emphasis is placed upon assessment as a product—for example, the assessment report. Assessment as product is dependent upon assessment as process. It is through the process that we come to know and understand those we serve. An assessment report presents the key learning and understanding that has been achieved through the assessment process.

> The assessment process and the product of the assessments that we conduct will be different every time.

The assessment process and the product of the assessment will be different every time. Every time we are engaged in assessment, be it with the same case or different cases that share character-istics, we will be different, the context will be different, and therefore the process and prod-uct will be different. Using a computer is a good analogy. When you turn on a program, a menu of tools appears at the top, which you then use to create a process for getting the job done. The sequence is never the same, yet it always results in a product—for example, a written report, a PowerPoint presentation, or a spreadsheet.

Assessment is Both Ongoing and Discrete or Defined

We can never say that we are done with assessment in any type of case. Assessment is a critical step in planning and it must precede all other steps and tasks. Therefore, it is possible and helpful to distinguish some beginning and end points for assessment. The concept of assessment as both ongoing and discrete or defined is difficult to convey.

> Assessment is a critical step in planning and it must precede all other steps and tasks.

When you are involved with a case you are always in inquiry about some aspect of practice—for example: What is going on? What can be done? However, at some point practitioners need to declare their formulation based on the assessment and generate a written plan.

For example, imagine that you are the public health nurse responsible for developing a program for young parents living in an inner city neighborhood who have recently had babies. The objective is to increase the parents' capacity to care appropriately for their infants. As you get to know the neighborhood and the parents and their children you are continually assessing and reassessing their needs, capacity, resources, and so on in order to develop a program that is meaningful and effective. While this could go on for months, at some point you have to work with what you have got and put together a plan for what you are going to do, for whom, when, where, with what, and so on. In defining the plan, it does not mean that you have stopped assessing, but rather, you have made a formulation with what your assessment has uncovered to date, while knowing that the formulation may need to change in the future.

Assessment is Multifaceted

The many aspects or elements of assessment that we have discussed are both complex and intertwined. This too is difficult to convey. For example, when we discuss the tasks of gathering and interpreting information, we do not want to leave the impression that there is an end to these tasks. As long as you are engaged in any aspect of practice, you are engaged in gathering and interpreting information.

> During assessment we are actually engaged in a cycle of gathering, analyzing, formulating, gathering, analyzing— ad infinitum.

During assessment we are actually engaged in a cycle of gathering, analyzing, formu-lating, gathering, analyzing, formulating—ad infinitum. For example, imagine that you are a key worker for Amity, a young woman who has been admitted to a residential pro-gram caring for youth with eating disorders. Before you even meet her, you are likely engaged in an assessment process and the gathering, analyzing, and formulating cycle. Through reading the case file or the admission/intake forms, you may obtain information about Amity's age, family, schooling, and medical history. You tease out some aspects that you find interesting and begin to formulate some ideas about what is going on for this young person. The first time you meet her, you gather more information about Amity and her family, school, friends, interests, hopes, and talents that allows you to check out your earlier formulations. You then refine or reorient your inquiry, gather more information, analyze it, and formulate ideas about what is going on. You keep engaging in this process while the focus of your inquiry shifts.

This process happens both in the moment, within the session and outside of the session, and upon reflection. To illustrate, during your time together, Amity tells you that she doesn't want anything to do with her parents. Your in-the-moment analysis and formulation is that there are parent-child issues, and you explore this further with her in an effort to understand more about what is behind her comment. Later on, when she asks if her parents have phoned today to see how she is doing and you respond, "No, not yet," she stops talking, casts her eyes downward, and then looks out the window. A small tear forms in each eye that she quickly wipes away as she turns back to you and asks, "How long has Jacquie (another program participant) been here?" The apparent inconsistency between her statement and her behavior adds more information to your assessment and suggests new areas for inquiry. The in-the-moment assessment informs the sessional assessment that informs the broader assessment and vice versa (see Figure 5.2).

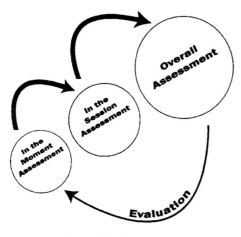

Figure 5.2.   Assessment.

Assessment is Influenced by the Context for Practice

The context for our practice, including assessment, at the very least influences the path we take when we do an assessment. In many cases it goes beyond influencing and actually dictates or directs aspects of what we do, what we consider, and how we interpret information. For example, the organization may specify (through legislation, policy, procedures, and standards) the time frame and time allocation for the assessment, who must undertake it, who must be involved or contacted, how information will be obtained, the weight or significance that will be given to information, and the format and length of the assessment report. To illustrate, an assessment will be completed in two weeks. During this time, the case file will be reviewed, and the youth, the youth's parents and stepfather, key worker, psychiatrist, and school counselor will be interviewed for their views on particular aspects of the situation (in response to specific questions). The recently completed psychiatric report will be a significant piece of information to be incorporated into the assessment report. The report will follow the standard format and be of no more than 10 pages in length.

In many jurisdictions the context for practice requires that certain processes take place in order to complete an assessment and formulate or implement a plan. These processes include case conferencing, integrated case management, family group conferencing, and healing circles, to name but a few. The client's context is also a significant contributor to the determination of the assessment process. For example, if a family is in crisis and an immediate response is required, the assessment process must be guided by the urgency of the situation.

Assessment is Something We Often Just Do

To be intentional in assessment requires us to have some explicit understanding about how we do assessment that goes beyond specific procedures we might employ or tools we might use. It is both a challenge and an opportunity to reflect upon what this "doing" is about. For example, what frameworks and models do we use, how do we decide what to inquire about and how, what information do we give weight to, what triggers us to probe more deeply into some areas and not others, and what do we do when faced with inconsistent and incongruent information?

There are Multiple Frameworks for Assessment

Because there are many different frameworks for assessment, you may (and likely do) operate within multiple frameworks. To return to the computer analogy, think about the drop-down menus in computer programs. When you decide that you need to do some formatting, you click on the Format option and a menu of choices is presented. You may then choose a particular subset on this menu, which in turn gives you another array of options, and so on.

To illustrate how this applies to assessment in a child welfare context, use the following as your starting point: Is the child at risk of harm if she continues to reside with her parents? Initially, you may apply a risk assessment framework, whereby you will obtain some information and likely discover some new areas of inquiry, such as, Does this family have a support network that they can draw on as needed? With this idea in mind, you may tap into a social systems framework or family assets/capacity model to help you assess the family's networks and capacities. If you have questions about the relationship between the parents and power dynamics, you may draw on yet another framework to help you in the assessment. You are, in effect, jumping from menu to menu and making choices that allow you to work within multiple frameworks simultaneously.

To illustrate using a mental health context: Is this youth likely to harm or kill herself if she is released from the emergency ward in her current state? Initially you will likely assess her mental health status in the moment using the records, techniques, and tools available to you. For example: Has the youth made a suicide attempt? Is the youth having a psychotic episode? Is she on or off her medication? You may draw on the expertise of others in the hospital to do their assessment and use information from her mental health history. The findings may lead you to identify other topics for consideration such as, Where are the youth's parents and are they willing and able to take charge of and monitor their child? This might require that you draw on a framework for assessing family capacity.

Oftentimes, we are not even conscious of the frameworks that we are using; we just do it. However, it is helpful to pay attention to the frameworks we use so that we can reflect upon how they work for us. We have also found it helpful to pay attention to any discomfort that we feel in the assessment process. Our discomfort may reveal the need to rethink which frameworks we use, to go in a different direction or delve deeper, to add to our repertoire, or to consult with others to gain different perspectives.

Assessment Demands Compassion

Having compassion is being inclined to help, to restore harmony, to care, and perhaps even to love.

Very often in professional training we are encouraged to separate the professional from our personal lives as if they are two worlds, and in so doing drop the compassion or feelings. Good assessments require real compassion. To not be compassionate is to be perfunctory, to do the job, to fill out the forms, and to make things happen. However, perfunctory services lack passion, lack the appreciation or the expression of appreciation for the pain and struggle, and lack the determination required to ensure the plan is implemented, monitored, and successful. Our feelings parallel and accompany our thoughts and actions. If we do not attend to our feelings we risk ignoring an important resource for assessment. Feelings inform our sympathies, sensitivities, awareness, and emotional response. In essence, compassion informs our assessment by complementing the information provided through the intellect.

We Take Ourselves Everywhere We Go

As discussed in Chapter 3, health and social services work is personal work. We take ourselves and our attitudes, beliefs, values, experiences, and skills everywhere we go, including into the assessment process. Understanding self as an emergent practitioner helps us to be aware of the frameworks and models we use, our process for inquiry, what information we give weight to, and what affects us in the different contexts of practice. We believe, for example, it is crucial to give voice to the people we serve so that their issues, concerns, needs, capacities, and capabilities are expressed and attended to in planning. However, as practitioners we come into our practice through different paths. Our different life experiences influence the kinds of questions we ask, how we ask them, how we listen, how we respond, what formulations we make, and who we engage to gather information.

> Consider assessment as a multifaceted and context-influenced process of information gathering and interpretation. It is a delicate process of discovery that requires tuning in beyond what might be immediately apparent.

To summarize, we invite you to consider assessment as a multifaceted and context-influenced process of information gathering and interpretation. It is a delicate process of discovery that requires tuning in beyond what might be immediately apparent. You must ascertain what is going on, what this means to the people involved (how do they understand and explain their situation), and what they want to be different or what they want different about their situation. By understanding the situation, as best we can, from the perspective of those living with it, we are better able to delineate what they might want changed.

We have noted that we often start at one place and end up in a completely different place through the process of inquiry. The question we often ask ourselves is: Does the collected information reveal a deep enough understanding to allow the practitioner to write a meaningful case plan? We have also noted that the process of assessment is never over as long as we are engaged in the case. Even when we have written a case plan we are still engaged in an assessment process. This process of discovery is depicted in Figure 5.3.

Early Assessment: To Take the Case or Not to Take the Case

One of the first assessment considerations is to decide whether or not to accept a referral or request to do something about a situation or for a person, family, community, organization, or system. The decision to accept, reject, or refer the case will be influenced or directed by the context for practice. For example, the organizational context may prescribe admission or acceptance criteria, which often relate to the purpose of the organization and its programs or services. For instance, an agency serving teen parents likely has admission criteria that set parameters for inclusion or exclusion based upon age and parental status, as well as the availability of space in the program. The agency may also set criteria such as attending school or a work placement training program, a child under the age of two years, a person on welfare, or parent is a ward of the state.

> Oftentimes the decision to accept or not accept a case is driven by the availability of appropriate resources.

Similarly, a service or advocacy agency or department may also set criteria for accepting or rejecting a case. Take, for example, a community outreach office with a mandate to serve people with mental illness who are either living on the streets or living intermittently in shelters. If this agency is asked to develop and deliver a program to help constituents find more stable housing, it will likely assess the feasibility of its participation on criteria relevant to its client group. This might include criteria for the availability and adequacy of its funding, the availability of resources to do the job well, and how the idea fits with the agency's mandate and priorities.

As these examples illustrate, some of the criteria for acceptance of a case may be established in statements of purpose or mandate, or in policies or procedures. Others may be developed at the time the situation presents itself. At times the criteria may even be difficult to define, although no less valid, as when a practitioner or an agency considers their gut reaction or intuitive response to a request or a proposal and acts accordingly.

Some criteria for acceptance or nonacceptance, and the associated procedures for coming to a decision, are more formal than others. For example, a quick telephone conversation may determine whether a contract worker will work with the client. However, in service agencies, procedures may include the need for a referral from a particular source, documentation of income or lack of income, or previous assessment information from a designated assessment center. Very often, specific documentation for acceptance is required. At the program, sector, or system

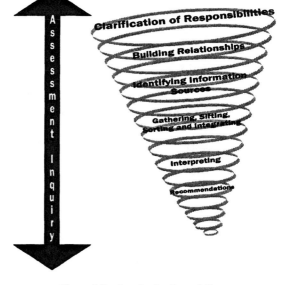

Figure 5.3.   Inquiry for Formulation.

level, procedures may involve receiving a formal request or proposal for assistance, reviewing the request in the context of other priorities, and reallocating financial and human resources to work on the situation.

Another context-based consideration is the resource context. Oftentimes the decision to accept or not accept a case is driven by the availability of appropriate resources, which, in our view, is a double-edged sword. On the one hand, we believe we should not accept cases that we are ill-prepared to serve. On the other hand, if we continue to exclude cases that don't fit the criteria or for whom we have no program, we may be maintaining the status quo and leaving many people in need out in the cold. We know of situations where long-term programs operate at 20 percent capacity. This means that many placements in the program are left vacant because the referrals don't fit program criteria. In these situations, questions should be asked, such as, Are the criteria appropriate? Does this program serve the needs of the people to whom we are responsible? What else is needed? How could we better address the needs of those not well served in this program? Instead, acting in accordance with the information obtained, irrelevant programs such as these are maintained. The important point here is not that there be a specific set of criteria established to determine whether a case will become a case, but rather that there are some clear and reasonable criteria (intentional and informed choice). Further, these criteria must be relevant and useful in order to be monitored and reflected upon on an ongoing basis. What this illustrates is that even before we engage in a comprehensive assessment and planning process on a case, there is a case to manage!

Of course, the flip side to a practitioner, agency, or system deciding whether or not to take a case is the client's determination of whether or not to participate. In some cases, clients have little choice when they are required, ordered, or mandated to participate in a program or service. However, even in these situations, clients retain the choice of how they will apply themselves, regardless of the expectations of the involved practitioners. Thus it is important to inform clients about the planning process, including what they might expect, who is involved, and what their rights and responsibilities are. This may be a mutual exploration of interests to determine the fit between the client and the practitioner or program, or between the people concerned about a particular issue and charged with planning to address it. Sometimes this is incorporated into an intake process.

The Process of Assessment

Assessment is a multifaceted process that involves

- Clarifying and negotiating responsibilities
- Building relationships
- Identifying information sources
- Gathering, sifting, sorting, and integrating information
- Interpreting information (formulating opinions, diagnoses, judgments) about troublesome behaviors, underlying needs, capabilities, and capacities
- Making recommendations for the point in time.

The practitioner's thinking, regardless of clinical or theoretical orientation, is not necessarily linear or sequential. For example, if after collecting information it is all determined to be relevant, then the integration and formulation of information may be the next step. If, however, all the information is not relevant, then sifting the relevant from the irrelevant may be the next step. The sequence of the process is repetitive within a single session and across sessions. Further, some steps will be more prominent or significant at certain times or within certain situations, while others will be less important.

> The mind gathers information, sifts and sorts it in light of certain criteria, and integrates it in order to formulate and select from a number of recommendations that are generated in the mind.

It might be useful to think of this process as how the mind works or plays with information. The mind holds and integrates information across sessions, and it does this whether it is managing assessment, service planning, or evaluation information. The mind engages in these steps throughout the assessment process, which begins when a case first becomes known to the practitioner and ends with a follow-up session or when the case work is completed. The mind gathers information, sifts and sorts it in light of certain criteria, and integrates it in order to formulate and select from a number of recommendations that are generated in the mind.

Before we examine each task in the assessment process and discuss the nature of their interconnectedness, consider the following cautions:

- The process is not necessarily linear or sequential.
- The different aspects of the process are interconnected and interdependent.
- The parts of the process are context influenced and dependent.
- All aspects of the process are influenced by who we are as practitioners and what we bring to the process.

Clarifying Responsibilities

Responsibilities should be clarified and negotiated early in the assessment process. This helps to situate the process of giving and receiving information and of formulating ideas and recommendations. That is, it serves to make clear what is being undertaken, who is involved, and what their roles are likely to be. It is particularly

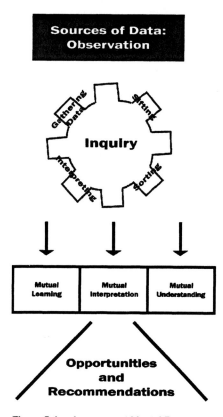

Figure 5.4.   Assessment Mental Processes.

> Roles and responsibilities should be clarified early in the assessment process.

important that clients (an individual, family, group, community, or organization) understand all aspects of assessment, as they are partners in the process. They should be apprised of who will be involved, for what purpose, what they can expect of those involved, how the assessment will be undertaken, and what is expected of them as clients.

In complex case situations and in different types of settings, many people may be involved in the assessment and planning process. Recall the example that was shared in Chapter 4 of Adele, who had 10 to 15 different professionals involved with her family, all with unique roles and functions defined by disciplines and organizational affiliation.

Recall also the example of the community worker concerned about the apparent disappearance of a number of street-involved people. Numerous people could have a role in assessing this situation, including police, parents and guardians, and advocates, to mention a few. The process of defining responsibilities provides an opportunity for various players to develop a shared understanding of who can offer what to the assessment process. We must also ensure that the delineation of responsibilities does not serve to keep us distant from the issues and from each other, and therefore unable to work collaboratively for understanding and generating what is possible.

> The participants in the assessment process must have some explicit understanding about roles and responsibilities and the client must share in this understanding.

In some situations, responsibilities are clearly defined in legislation, regulation, policy, procedures, service contracts, or job descriptions. In others, practitioners define their responsibilities in a set way according to their disciplinary or theoretical orientations, or their views of what is required or what they have to offer. In still other situations, there may be a mutual process of exploration and negotiation about who might do what, with roles defined by agreement. No matter how the responsibilities are defined and what they are, the participants in the assessment process must have some explicit understanding about roles and responsibilities, and the client must share in this understanding.

Building Relationships

Assessment is always undertaken in the context of relationships. For example, a licensing officer, responsible for ensuring that childcare settings deliver a consistent, high-quality service to children, may go into a center and have 30 minutes to complete her assessment. She may not know any of the staff members, parents, or children, or have any prior relationship with the other participants in the assessment process. However, as soon as she enters the building, she is engaged in a relationship with the other participants. What she does in the context of this relationship will influence the type and extent of information obtained and the course of the assessment.

> The initial relationship is instrumental in affecting an ongoing working relationship, and it requires careful management on the part of everyone involved.

In longer-term relationships there is often a "getting to know you" period of time; in some settings, this is labeled the intake period, the preliminary assessment phase, or the initial sessions. Typically, this involves a great deal of clarification, dealing with apprehensions and fears, and ensuring that expectations are understood going both ways, and that a mutual commitment to working together is made. This careful building of the initial relationship is instrumental in affecting an ongoing working relationship, and it requires careful management on the part of everyone involved.

Identifying Information Sources

Assessment is dependent upon information. This information comes from a wide range of sources, including

- People, such as the client, family members, friends, and others who know the client (e.g., teachers, caregivers, other service providers)
- Paper (e.g., case files, prior assessments, log entries)
- Direct observation.

Sometimes the sources of information are self-evident or clearly defined; other times, sources must be uncovered and may be difficult to access. In the earlier example of street-involved people who had disappeared, obvious sources include the police and other street people, but the latter may be unwilling to talk due to fear of breaking the street code of conduct or of being labeled as

> Sometimes the sources of information are self-evident or clearly defined; other times, sources must be uncovered and may be difficult to access.

an informant, or due to mistrust of authorities. Some information sources may be obvious yet still difficult to access as their identity is unknown, such as parents and former caregivers (e.g., foster parents). These and other sources may need to be sought out or uncovered. In other situations, sources are inaccessible; for example, case files of one agency (or even one branch of an agency) frequently cannot be used by practitioners from other settings. However, case conferencing, collaborative or joint assessment, or some other means may allow the information to be shared by those responsible for the files and the information they contain. As this example illustrates, the context not only affects sources of information but also their accessibility.

Direct observation is a key source of information. It is the systematic noting of behavior and involves the use of all the senses: watching, listening, smelling, touching, and tasting. It is necessary to ensure that observations are accurate (truthful) and described in precise language so that a representational or qualitative documentation of the behavior is described rather than a judgment about the observation. The best description is most likely to come from the client, although useful observations may be gathered from a wide range of sources, as illustrated by the following statement:

> John reports that no one likes him, his teacher states that he usually plays
> alone, his parents note that he does not bring friends home and is often in
> his room alone, and, when observed on the playground, he was by himself.

This set of observations is quite different from the judgment "John has no friends and is anti-social." In short, observations serve to open up possibilities for inquiry, whereas judgments close the inquiry down.

Gathering, Sifting, Sorting, and Integrating Information

When we gather information, we seek to understand what is going on, how people under-stand or make sense of their situation, and what they hope to have happen. We also identify, among other things, behaviors or situations that are troublesome to the people involved. Troublesome behaviors are complaints—that is, behaviors cited by the client as either trou-blesome or problematic, or something the client does not like. Troublesome behaviors can be seen, heard, smelled, or experienced. Individual examples might include smoking, drinking alcohol, being involved in the sex trade, beating up or raging at others, hiding out in the basement, not keeping oneself clean, or not sleeping, to mention a few. These signals are usually part of a set of troublesome behaviors and occur within a particular setting or set of circumstances. The set of behaviors may include drinking alcohol daily, losing one's temper for no apparent reason, experiencing physical symptoms of headaches and sore neck, feeling down and not wanting to go out and do things, and being unable to sleep through the night.

These behaviors may be defined by an individual, family, group, community, organiza-tion, or system. For example, parents might identify their child's bedwetting as a trouble-some behavior. A parent group might identify the high proportion of early school-leavers (dropouts) as troublesome. A community might identify the number of dogs left to run wild (and inflict bites, frighten children and the elderly, etc.) as troublesome. An organization might define the high incidence of stress leave amongst frontline staff as troublesome.

> Behaviors are only a starting point, alerting us to something that is bothersome and troublesome, and usually accompanied by a wish on the part of someone for change.

These behaviors may also have different meanings for different clients. For example, one client might regard his smoking as a dirty habit that he wants to stop, while another may experience smoking as a way to socialize and belong to a group. Yet another may express smoking as unhealthy and cite the fact that 50 percent of those who smoke will die from lung cancer.

Different parties to a troublesome situation may also attribute different meanings to the behaviors. For exam-ple, the high number of people on stress leave may represent different challenges to differ-ent members of the organization. For the program administrator, it may represent a problem of ensuring staff coverage and fulfilling licensing requirements. For the manager, it may mean the loss of a sense of team, and for the staff members on stress leave, it may represent a sense of defeat and despair. These different points of view can be probed and understood in depth by conducting an ongoing assessment. As noted earlier, these behav-iors are only a starting point, alerting us to something that is bothersome and troublesome, and usually accompanied by a wish on the part of someone for change.

The process of assessment is essentially the same regardless of the focus of attention. The theoretical and contextual frameworks used by practitioners define the focus of atten-tion. For example, if you embrace systems theory, you will be interested in learning who is included in the client's system and the nature of the relationships between them. If you are working with a family, you might ask questions that will uncover who each person includes or excludes within the family, who does what (roles), and how the family members align or distance themselves from each other. The types of questions you might ask include, What does Mom do when Dad and Tracy get into a fight? How often does Grandpa visit? How do each of you act differently when Grandpa comes? Picture drawing and family sculpting (where family members position each other in a human sculpture in order to illustrate relationships) are other techniques you might use.

The frameworks you use will be influenced by your worldview or perspective. For a program development example, imagine you are a family support worker hired to work within an inner city school in a large urban center. The children in the school come from a wide array of cultural backgrounds. The vast majority of their families live in poverty, English is not their first language, and many of them have learning challenges. Your job is to build bridges between the school, the families, and the resources within the community. You know what some of the problems are, but not what to do about them. What information would you seek out and why? How would you gather information that would allow you to develop goals and a plan?

If you operate within a belief system that emphasizes community health, then you may use a capacity framework to guide your information gathering. You will likely seek out information from members of the school community (students, parents, community leaders within different cultural groups) and service providers who seem most connected to the community. Your questions will focus on understanding what the community is like and uncovering its assets and strengths, as well as its challenges, from the perspective of those living within it. Students might be asked:

- What do you do after school and during school vacations?
- What would you like to be able to do after school and during school vacations?
- If you need some help with a problem, where do you go for help?

  Community leaders might be asked:
- Where do families go together to worship, celebrate events, be with other families, and so on?
- What happens when families are having difficulties?
- Who do they turn to for help?
- What is working well in the community?
- What would you like to see grow and develop to make your community a better place?

In gathering information about a problem, practitioners may work with multiple frameworks—either simultaneously or sequentially. These might guide the types of questions that are asked, how the questions are framed, and who is included in the inquiry, as well as how the information is organized and interpreted. Practitioners employ different perspectives and frames as required. As one condition arises, practitioners respond to cues that lead to certain formulations and approaches. As these cues fade, their focus shifts to new cues that emerge and require a different frame. Additional examples of frameworks for data collection are included in Appendix B. Our purpose here is to encourage you to use a framework (or frameworks) to do assessments and to be aware of its influence on the way in which you gather and use information.

> As practitioners collect information, they sort the relevant from the irrelevant and integrate the information so that it is useful for making the next move and for planning overall.

In the context of assessment, practitioners take in information from as many different sources as possible. The client may say one thing but do something quite different within

The issues, and their meaning and significance, may shift over the course of the assessment.

a session. This situation allows practitioners to collect additional information in order to judge which data set is more accurate or representative of the client. Practitioners may check out the data set with their client and engage the client in formulating what it means and what significance it has to them.

As practitioners collect information, they sort the relevant from the irrelevant and integrate the information so that it is useful for making the next move and for planning overall. This fluid nature of gathering, sifting, sorting, and integrating information means that assessments do not always go smoothly or in a straight line. As a result, the issues, and their meaning and significance, may shift over the course of the assessment.

Interpreting Information

Interpretation, or meaning-making, is the attributing or ascribing of meaning to information that has been gathered, sifted, sorted, and integrated.

Interpretation, or meaning-making, is the attributing or ascribing of meaning to information that has been gathered, sifted, sorted, and integrated. This results in opinions that identify what is going on (including, but often going beyond, the identified troublesome behaviors), the meaning attributed to the situation by the people involved, what underlying needs might be emerging, and what might be the appropriate next action. It is integrated with an understanding about the capabilities and capacities of the client (individual, family, group, community, organization, or system). Generally, we engage in interpretation using one or more sets of criteria. These criteria give greater weight to some information, and influence the way that we package the information. These criteria are grounded in our theoretical orientations, for example, the behaviorist is judging current behaviors on past learning, while the systems therapist is assessing patterns in the family.

The process of interpretation may then be a joint effort between the client and the practitioners charged with figuring out what to do.

Criteria may be defined or influenced by the therapeutic milieu, program or organizational priorities, and other elements deeply embedded in the context. Criteria may also be discussed by, defined by, or mutually established with the client. To illustrate, an organization seeking to address a lack of interagency collaboration may undertake to interpret information using criteria that has been defined by the client (i.e., locate the barriers to information sharing and determine whether people, procedures, attitudes, or something else is creating or maintaining these barriers). The process of interpretation may then be a joint effort between the client and the practitioners charged with figuring out what to do. However, regardless of whether the client defines the criteria or actively interprets the information, it is critical that the meaning the client gives to information is understood and accounted for within the interpretation. This is another aspect of practice that is difficult to convey. Therefore, rather than walk you through an example and give you our interpretation, we will describe how we think interpretation works.

Interpretation is a translation or meaning given to the collection of information in order to understand and explain the situation at hand.

We have already suggested the need for an atmosphere of inquiry. More specifically, we think the pathway of inquiry requires a process of mutual inquiry (see Figure 5.5). Mutual inquiry involves identifying the sources of information and then analyzing the information. The analysis is the process of gathering, sifting, sorting, and integrating information in preparation for interpretation. Interpretation is a translation or meaning given to the collection of information in order to understand and explain the situation at hand. The objective of mutual inquiry is to gain an understanding in relation to each other, so that an appropriate plan can be generated together. What we mean by mutual is that each has a perception of the sources of information. By sharing our perceptions and working with the information, we achieve a shared perception of the information, which includes a mutual understanding of where there is disagreement.

> By sharing our perceptions and working with the information, we achieve a shared perception of the information, which includes a mutual understanding of where there is disagreement.

We suggest that the assessment pathway of inquiry is one in which the client and practitioner learn together what the collected information and observations mean. The first step is to become aware of the collected information and observations; this involves a mutual

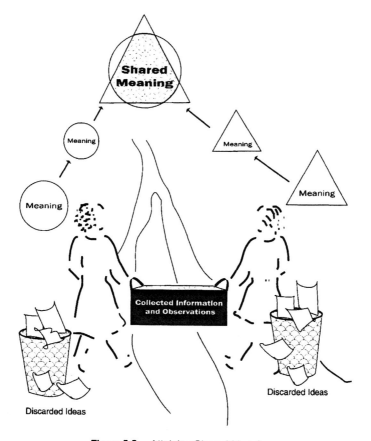

Figure 5.5.   Attaining Shared Meaning.

consciousness of what has been shared. Once the mutual consciousness is apparent, those involved move towards a mutual understanding of what the information and observations mean, including where there is agreement, disagreement, similarities, and differences. This understanding comes through the attribution of meaning by those involved; that is, those involved have assigned an equivalent meaning to the same sources of data. Think of it as co-creating a shared picture. Within the picture, there may be a section where there is little agreement between the client and the practitioner, but there is a mutual recognition of any disagreement. Figure 5.5 portrays the critical sequence of learning together and having knowledge or understanding through the attribution of meaning.

Although the process of mutual learning happens in split seconds, it may take hours, if not days, to get to the point of having a mutual picture of the whole situation. And, when this point is reached it is a temporary state; you are operating within a larger culture of inquiry, and within a culture of inquiry, more observations are bound to come to light, hence the ongoing opportunity for new meaning and understanding. For example, to return to Figure 5.4, we first consider sources of information, which evolve throughout the learning process. However, even if the sources of information stay the same, a different analysis process may bring about different learning, new meaning, and different understanding that, in turn, would yield different opportunities from those first thought possible.

Throughout the assessment, and indeed through the completion of the case, the practitioner interprets information for assessment and planning. Assessments are usually mutually agreed to—even if not mutually generated by the practitioner and the client—but to what extent varies according to one's theoretical orientation and beliefs about planning.

Interpretation and creating meaning involve reflection, and therefore perhaps more time than we have to give. It's like cooking soup and, as everyone knows, soup must be cooked slowly. However, the more accurately goals are formulated, the more relevant they are. Sometimes difficult cases have nothing to do with the clients and how they behave or their situation, and everything to do with our assessment process. When our process has been flawed or incomplete, or has taken us down the wrong path, our interpretations will be off, therefore our assessment will be off, and therefore our plan will be off. Often, when this happens, practitioners intervene in ways that are not significant to the client, make no difference to the client's change progress, or may actually cause the client harm.

Making Recommendations for the Point in Time

> The final step in assessment is the generation of recommendations.

At some point, the practitioner and, hopefully, the client will determine that the process of information gathering, sifting, sorting, integrating, and interpreting has yielded sufficient relevant information and mutual understanding for recommendations to be made. The final step in assessment is the generation of recommendations. These are statements about the issues for the client, what might be done, and how to monitor progress. The recommendations should make inherent sense to anyone who reads them because they are derived from the information gathered and generated out of the meaning given to the information by the practitioner and the client. Basically, what is being recommended is a way to look at or think about the client and her issues. Out of these recommendations comes the formulation of the case plan, including needs, goals, service actions, and an evaluation plan.

To help you better understand this process, we offer the following account of an assessment as described by the supervising nurse in an organization:

> I have had a working and personal relationship with Mary for the past 22 years. I was her supervisor in a previous setting and have supervised her in this setting for the past year and a half. I would describe our working relationship as positive, straightforward, and mutually trustworthy. I consider her to be one of the best employees I have ever worked with. I respect her capabilities in reflecting, problem solving, and getting the job done. We appear to have a mutual affection and respect for each other because we have similar capabilities and values.
>
> I first noticed that Mary was not meeting deadlines and expectations about six months before I said anything to her. The unmet deadlines and expectations were showing up in her personal life with regard to her children, family issues, employment pressure because of financial problems, and professional growth and training initiatives, and in terms of a critical project that we agreed to do together. These multiple sources of data alerted me to the fact that there was a problem for her that was becoming a problem for me. The initial troublesome behavior was incomplete work or work that did not meet her usual standard. It was this capacity to meet a high standard that I valued and wanted on this new project. Other indicators that were showing up included both of us feeling frustrated, both of us becoming tired and looking stressed, and a scattered approach on her part to keep all the saucers in the air. We had a problem.
>
> We met a couple of times and considered all these sources of information and began to unravel what was happening and what it meant. I shared with her my observations and probed with her what was happening and what it meant to her. She confirmed that the problems that were showing up in different aspects of her life were interrelated and were contaminating each other to the point that she felt like it was all falling down. She also agreed that how she was presenting was incongruent with how she saw herself.
>
> We probed each aspect of her life and the presenting troublesome behaviors. In exploring these she reported her experiences and her perspectives on what they meant, and I would respond by suggesting that perhaps there was more. For example, initially she talked about her feelings of personal anxiety and frustration, and physical symptoms of not feeling well. This kind of experience takes her to a place of pulling away, feeling out of control, and taking flight. I suggested to her that perhaps by discussing these issues it made explicit that indeed things were out of control and that she was experiencing "being out of control," and I asked her what that meant. She responded by saying that for her it was a shaming experience because she was not able to live up to how she should be, which is to be strong, figure it out, and work harder. The fundamental belief that she identified is that if she just followed these rules, everything would be okay. The fact that she could not handle everything meant that she had been caught at being out of control and was therefore a failure. I suggested further that it sounded like she had to do it alone, that she couldn't ask for help, and that she couldn't renegotiate time lines as that would make explicit the failure and she would then wonder what others thought of her. She agreed.
>
> This process of examining the information and making meaning from it took some time and each session revealed new awareness for both of us as to what was happening, what it meant for both of us, and therefore what was possible. We agreed that we wanted to continue on the project but not under the present circumstances. This was a critical confirmation of our relationship and the importance of resolving the issue. Together we formulated a plan whereby what we decided to do was nested within our mutual understanding of what we needed and how we wanted that to look.

Needs: Mary and I want to continue our relationship and succeed in this project. Our commitment to this was reconfirmed. Mary needs to be out from under the pressure of taking the leadership in the project as she has too much other pressure in her life at this point. Mary and I need a working relationship that allows for collaboration that includes telling the truth and renegotiating the plan as we go. We also need to be clear that while we expect a great deal from each other, we do not expect perfection!

Goals: Mary and I will complete the project to our mutual satisfaction by January 2003. Mary will not feel burdened by the project, throughout the project. We will tell each other the truth and renegotiate the work as we go along, focusing on getting the project done. Mary will gain an understanding of how her family of origin and other previous relationships continue to show up in many areas of her life.

Service Plan: I will take the lead role in the project. We will call each other daily and check on how it is going. Daily plans will be negotiated as we go along. We will ask each other how we are feeling about what we are doing, and what we need from each other on each day. Mary will continue her therapy in order to sort out personal issues related to her family of origin.

Evaluation: We will monitor daily how we are feeling and tell each other. We will assess how we feel about the finished product and whether we met the deadline. We will not use the completion of the project as a definition of who we are, nor will we use it to define our relationship. There will be no recording of the monitoring, although it will be acknowledged that there is no longer a problem.

Summary

To summarize, the planning process framework simply identifies the fundamental need for an assessment to inform planning. No guidelines are suggested beyond that of being conscious about the frameworks, strategies, and techniques that you employ. Ultimately, assessment is a process of continual revision:

test – operate – test – operate – test – operate – evaluate!

> Your assessment is a statement of your understanding of the client's situation that is reflected in a case plan formulation.

Because assessment is not a series of predictable steps, you must determine your own maps, frames, and criteria for interpretations or meaning-making that will help you develop an understanding of the client's situation. In the final analysis, your assessment is a statement of your understanding of the client's situation that is reflected in a case plan formulation.

Case Plan Formulations

Assessment provides us with what we need to formulate case plans. We use a planned-change model as a frame for the formulation of case plans. The model has four core elements:

1. Need(s)
2. Goal(s)
3. Service action(s)
4. Evaluation.

It serves us well whether we are engaged in plan formulation for an individual, family, group, community, organization, or system. As illustrated in Figure 5.6, the elements are represented in a linear way; however, as with everything discussed within this section, the actual application of the model is far from being linear. We will now discuss each element and the way in which the model may be used in practice.

Identifying Needs

Needs, and therefore need statements, involve circumstances that require a course of action. Very often in planning we think about the course of action before thinking through the purpose for the action or change. We believe that the way in which practitioners define needs relates to how they think

Figure 5.6.   Inquiry for Plan Formulation.

about change and what they think needs to be changed. Recall our earlier discussions on theoretical orientations for behavior change, as well as other perspectives about what is important in practice. Changing behavior and circumstances for individuals, groups, families, and communities can be important, as can being socially

> The way in which practitioners define needs relates to how they think about change and what they think needs to be changed.

responsible or ensuring equity for all, especially those oppressed and unaware. Therefore, before using this model, you must define your purpose in practice. You may also want to consider aspects of change at all levels of practice. For example, working with individuals may have a different focus from working with communities. When working with individuals, the focus of change might be on behavior change or changing the situation; in focusing on individuals, needs may be defined in terms of developmental theories. If you use a developmental framework, your ideas about needs may be similar to the following formulation.

Needs are physiological, emotional, social, and spiritual requirements for the well-being of an individual, family, or group. They can represent an ongoing requirement, or something that is required to address a deficit or what is missing, in order for the person to be in a state of well-being, or happy and healthy. Needs for individuals within a community, organization or system relate to identity and purpose, survival, growth, and/or transition. Humans and their social systems (including families, groups, and communities) are complex entities that have different kinds of needs.

As physical beings we have physiological needs—that is, needs related to health and growth. As emotional beings we have psychological needs for safety, security, love, and self-identity or sense of self. We need to express authentic feelings for self and others and have that reciprocated by others within our relationships. As social beings we need to be involved with others, have a sense of belonging to family and community, and have skills to relate to and communicate with others while at work and play. Our spiritual needs

Area of Need	Need Statement Example
Physical	*Individual:* Tomas needs to learn skills that will allow him to ensure his physical health in the context of his disability and to maintain his independence. *Family:* The Milne family needs to understand and overcome the alcoholism that has spread across the three generations of living members.
Emotional	*Individual:* Elaine needs to accept herself in terms of being a warm, caring human being rather than link her acceptance to success performance at work and school. *Family:* The Macintosh/Jones family needs to allow for each member of the family to grieve in his or her own way over the loss of Mom in order to recreate their family life without her.
Social	*Individual:* Geoff needs to establish social relationships with peers and interact with them as equals. *Family:* The Singh family needs to establish a social support network that is accepting of their cultural traditions and priorities while also assisting them in coping with their child with autism.
Spiritual	*Individual:* Pam needs to find ways to express and nurture her developing spiritual interests. *Family:* The Timms family needs to accept that different family members have different spiritual needs and that the choice some members have made to move away from the family's traditional church does not represent a rejection of the family.

Table 5.2. Examples of Need Statements

are also now being recognized and attended to in health and social service practice. Spiritual needs represent an aspect of the self that is distinct from the physical self and embodies our character, or elevated qualities of the mind. Spirituality can be manifested through religious affiliations, belief in God and/or in the soul, or meditative rituals that support the spiritual self.

Examples of need statements relating to individuals within families, groups, and communities are presented in Table 5.2.

Needs are also manifested within groups, communities, organizations, and systems. As with individuals, you need to be clear about your theoretical orientation for organization or system change. There are cybernetic or information system theories for organizations, developmental theories for organizations and systems, and more current learning organization theories for change. Examples of need statements relating to groups, communities, organizations, and systems are presented in Table 5.3.

These statements of need represent what the people involved in the situation feel is significant for them. They are a reflection of their needs, rather than needs defined by practitioners alone or by others who hold the purse strings. To our dismay, we have seen need statements based on what the practitioner thinks is important (although the client does not) or framed so that the practitioner can use a favorite intervention, such as a narrative approach or behavior modification (which may or may not be relevant to the client).

Area of Need	Need Statement Example
Developmental	*Community:* The gay/lesbian/bisexual community within this institution needs to achieve acceptance by the mainstream community such that people who are gay, lesbian, or bisexual are not discriminated against within the institution. The dominant culture within this institution needs to learn and understand the differences of gays, lesbians, two-spirited, bisexual, and queer members of our community.
Cybernetic	*Organization:* The organization needs practitioners who can identify, monitor, and use information for decision-making and planning.
Learning Organization	*Group:* The group needs to identify its strengths, weaknesses, and capacities in light of the turnover. *Organization:* The organization needs to create a shared vision and learn together how to achieve that vision.

Table 5.3. Examples of Need Statements

An example of the former is "Kate needs to learn household management skills, including cooking and cleaning, in order to provide a better environment for the baby." The problem with this need statement is that household-management skills are not significant to Kate at this time. She is struggling with the challenge of caring for a newborn, feeling ill-prepared to care for him and socially isolated. Her needs include getting some assurance that she can provide adequate care for her baby, reorienting her thinking from "I can't do this" to "I can and I will do this" and reconnecting with her friends.

An example of the latter faulty approach is "Andy needs to participate in an anger management program." This is a statement of strategy, not need. The underlying need is that Andy needs to develop ways to manage and appropriately express his anger. Although an anger management course may be a reasonable intervention, the course itself does not represent a need—even if the practitioner has just completed a workshop on how to do this. Practitioners who define needs in this way may, in fact, fear not being able to address the client's real needs. However, in our view, it is not helpful to the client.

Goals and Goal Setting

Goals are behavioral statements of how the individual or individuals will be at the end of a specified period of time. They specify the different behaviors to be in place, or the change in circumstances, and represent the needs, therefore reflecting the theoretical orientation to change. Put another way, goals are ends or objectives the client is to achieve. They may express how the client (individual, family, group, community, organization, or system) will be after treatment—that is, how the client will look, feel, and act differently—or they may identify the next stage of development for an organization. It is important to identify the behavioral difference that captures the real change needed and wanted by the client. If you and the client do not know the desired outcome, it is unlikely that the outcome will be realized.

> Goals are behavioral statements of how the individual or individuals will be at the end of a specified period of time.

Goal statements do not always pick up on troublesome behaviors, but sometimes they can. The key to identifying accurate goals is to understand that there must be a relationship amongst troublesome behaviors, assessment, needs, and goals. Although assessment begins with troublesome behaviors and may end up with need and goal statements similar to these behaviors, the goal statements themselves can be very different from the troublesome behaviors and needs. For example, the goal for Elaine might read: For Elaine to experience and accept that she is warm and caring and that her success experiences at work and school have been more important for her parents than for her, by September 16, 2002. Alternatively, it might read: For Elaine to move out of her parents' house, by September 1, 2002, find a new job that brings her joy and pleasure by December 2002, and decide whether to marry George in spite of her parent's objections, by April 2003. Both goal plans could represent the change that Elaine wants in her life, yet they read very differently.

Table 5.4 provides examples of goals set relative to the needs identified for individuals, families, groups, communities, and organizations in the preceding section on needs.

Need Statements	Goal Statement Examples
Individual: Tomas needs to learn skills that will allow him to ensure his physical health in the context of his disability and to maintain his independence.	Tomas will learn necessary self-care and transfer skills, the risks and indicators of insufficient care, and appropriate responses to the indicators, by February 2003. Tomas will independently maintain his health status for a six-month period, by August 2003. Tomas will resume his independent living, by September 2003.
Individual: Elaine needs to accept herself in terms of being a warm, caring human being rather than link her acceptance to success performance at work and school.	Elaine will describe herself as a caring human being, without qualifying it with any reference to school or work performance, by June 2004. Elaine will reduce the number of stress-related symptoms (headaches, loss of sleep, feeling low, no fun in her life) that she experiences as a result of worrying about her school and work, by April 2003.
Individual: Geoff needs to establish relationships with peers and interact with them as equals.	Geoff will establish a friendship with one person, by May 2002. Geoff will report that he has a friend that he cares about, enjoys being with, and knows cares about him, by October 2002.
Individual: Pam needs to find ways to express and nurture her developing spiritual interests.	Pam will identify the ways that she would like to pursue and express her interest in spirituality, by March 2002. Pam will be able to discuss her spirituality, by December 2003.
Family: The Milne family needs to understand and overcome the alcoholism that has spread across the three generations of living members.	The Milne family will be able to explain the alcohol abuse that has spread across the three generations, by September 2003. The Milne family members will be able to discuss and explain different ways of thinking about addiction, by September 2004. The Milne family members will generate a plan to "kick" the use of alcohol in their family, by December 2004. *Continued*

Table 5.4.   Examples of Goal Statements

Need Statements	Goal Statement Examples
Family: The Macintosh/ Jones family needs to allow for each member of their family to grieve in his or her own way over the loss of Mom in order to recreate their family life without her.	The family will rethink how their family will operate now that Mom is dead, and will not forget her, by January 2003. Family members will take on new roles that will be negotiated as a family, by April 2003. Family members will be able to discuss Mom without family incidents and reactions, by June 2003.
Family: The Singh family needs to establish a social support network that is accepting of their cultural traditions and priorities while also assisting them in coping with their child with autism.	The Singh family will have someone they trust, can talk to, and can seek support and advice from, by October 2003. The Singh family will feel less shame about having a child with a disability, by October 2004.
Family: The Timms family needs to accept that the different family members have different spiritual needs and that the choice some members have made to move away from the family's traditional church does not represent a rejection of the family.	The Timms family will accept Emily and Brian's decision to no longer attend the family church, by January 2003. Emily and Brian will accept that the other members of their family want to continue in the churches, by January 2003. All will go to their separate churches without nasty comments and snide remarks about what is happening, by January 2004.
Organization: The organization needs practitioners who can identify, monitor, and use information for decision making and planning.	The organization will have an information system that allows practitioners to track clients and keep an accurate and up-to-date case file. On-line files will be used for decision making and planning on a regular basis.
Community: The gay/lesbian/bisexual community within this institution needs to achieve acceptance by the mainstream community such that people who are gay, lesbian, or bisexual are not discriminated	Community members will be able to use the language of sexual minority members within discussions, by December 2003. An equity policy and a plan for promoting equality of rights and anti-discrimination will be developed by the gay/lesbian/bisexual community in collaboration with other marginalized groups, by December 2003. Community members will jointly decide what research plan will serve their interests with regard to understanding sexual minorities, by March 2004.

Continued

Table 5.4. *Continued*

Need Statements	Goal Statement Examples
against within the institution. The dominant culture within this institution needs to learn and understand the differences of gays, lesbians, two-spirited, bisexual, and queer members of our community.	The community will develop and present a policy and plan to the institutional administration for ratification, by March 2004.
Group: The group needs to identify its strengths, weaknesses and capacities in light of the turnover.	The group will identify the strengths, weaknesses, and capacities of the members of the group, as well as by the collective, by June 2003. A new recruitment strategy, aimed at engaging practitioners who are creative, open-minded, and energetic, will be put in place, by September 2003.
Learning Organization: The organization needs to create a shared vision and learn together how to achieve that vision.	Five new practitioners will be recruited, by December 2003. The organization and new recruits will create a shared vision and generate a plan on how to achieve that vision, by June 2004.

Table 5.4. *Continued*

Note that there may be more than one goal identified for each need. There could also be one goal that addresses multiple needs. Goals may be process oriented, as in those including phrases such as "develop a plan," "obtain support," or "conduct a meeting." Although these goals may look similar to service actions (to be discussed later), they are still statements about where an individual, family, group, community, organization, or system wants to be at a point in time.

Guidelines for Goals

Guidelines for goals are related either to the assessment process or to the technology of goal setting. Guidelines related to the assessment process include setting goals that are

- Related to client's need(s)
- Possible, given the client's present level of functioning and capacity
- Realistic, given the client's present level of functioning and capacity.

Obviously, these guidelines require an assessment of the client's capabilities and capacities if the goal statements are to reflect what is realistic relative to the client's capabilities and current level of functioning. Goal statements also reflect the client's capacity—that is, what can be achieved by the client within a specified period of time, given the nature and the length of service being provided. In other words, goals are related to the client's capacity within the service context.

In terms of setting technically accurate goals, goals must be precise, with complete descriptions of how the client is to present or what the client is to be like, when the goal is achieved. Ideally, anyone reading the goal should know by observing the client if the goal has been achieved. The following guidelines apply whether the goals are about individuals, groups, families, or organizations:

> Goals must be precise and complete descriptions of how the client is to present, or what the client is to be like, when the goal is achieved.

- Write statements that describe what the client does, not what the practitioner does. For example, "Tomas will learn necessary self-care and transfer skills, the risks and indicators of insufficient care, and appropriate responses to the indicators, by February 2003," not "The home care nurse will teach Tomas self-care and transfer skills, by February 2003."
- Write statements that specify an outcome or result rather than a process. For example, "The Singh family will have someone they trust, can talk to, and can seek support and advice from, by October 2003," not "The family support worker will help the Singhs find supportive connections in their community." The latter is a statement of intent by the practitioner to engage in a process and is, therefore, not a goal statement.
- Statements that involve a change in a client's attitude or some other state not open to direct observation require the specification of observable behaviors either within the goal statement itself or within the statement of indicators developed for the purposes of evaluating progress. For example, the goal statement "The Timms family will accept Emily and Brian's decision to no longer attend the family church, by January 2003," uses the term "accept," which is subject to varying interpretations. This goal could be clarified by stating it as: "The Timms family will reinstate Emily and Brian's allowances and privileges and no longer make the receipt of these things conditional upon their regular attendance at church." Alternatively, the indicators for this goal could specify behavioral changes such as "All family members will go to their separate churches without nasty comments or snide remarks."

Goals only come out of a complete and thorough assessment. When you have difficulty setting goals, it is probably due to an incomplete assessment or, at the very least, an incomplete examination, translation, interpretation, or meaning-making of the problem. Therefore, be sure to review the assessment, particularly the interpretation or meaning-making of the client's situation and the statement of needs.

The goal-setting process is similar, regardless of the nature of the service action or whom we are setting goals for—that is, individuals, families, groups, communities, organizations, or systems. Basically, all the relevant information gathered through assessment is shared with key persons, and the different perspectives and needs of those involved or affected are identified. Goals are determined in light of these needs and of where it makes sense to begin. As we will discuss later, there is no linear relationship between needs and goals. Goals are those aspects of self and others that represent the focus of change—that is, what is to be different or the desired outcome for this situation, person, organization, or family.

Service Action

Once an assessment is undertaken and needs and goals are established, service action plans can be developed. These plans specify what will be done, by whom, how, and when. They also often specify what will indicate that the plan is relevant and effective.

> Service action plans specify what will be done, by whom, how, and when.

Being clear about the needs and goals makes planning for service action more straightforward. Service options should not be considered because of availability but rather because of their potential for delivering the results (goal success) desired. Each service action plan is best negotiated and generated with those to be served. Relevant plans guide the nature of the practitioner's activities and interventions in all aspects of their practice with their clients.

> The service action plan sets out the interventions or strategies to be used to bring about the change desired by the clients.

The service action plan sets out the interventions or strategies to be used to bring about the change desired by clients. They are behavioral statements of what the practitioner or agency plans and does to assist clients in achieving their goals. Very simply, the service action plan is a statement of assigned program—that is, the nature of the service, interventions, strategies, or methods to be provided within the program. This statement demystifies the therapeutic process and turns it into an activity statement that can be planned, articulated, and monitored by the practitioner, as well as by the clients. It also identifies the treatment or service procedures—whether overall program, sessional, or in-the-moment interventions—that will be implemented to move the client towards the goals. Table 5.5 provides some examples of service action for the needs and goals that were established earlier.

Service action statements can identify both overall service actions and sessional service actions. Overall service actions are statements that describe the general service to be provided—for example, family therapy, group home, foster care, or residential treatment. Sessional service actions are statements of what is to be done during a particular time with the client—for example, during a home visit, the use of role play.

An example of an overall and a sessional service action statement related to a goal is given in Table 5.6.

Having developed a service action plan does not mean that planning is finished. Plans are point-in-time statements and will need to be reviewed and modified over time.

Evaluation

> Evaluation is the systematic collection of information on goal indicators and/or service actions for the purpose of decision making and planning.

Evaluation is the systematic collection of information on goal indicators and/or service actions for the purpose of decision making and planning. Basically, evaluation is the monitoring of service delivery and goal progress in order to determine whether we did what we said we

Goal Statement Examples	Service Action Examples
Tomas will learn necessary self-care and transfer skills, the risks and indicators of insufficient care, and appropriate responses to the indicators, by February 2003.	The home care nurse will teach Tomas self-care and transfer skills. Tomas' physician and the home care nurse will discuss the risks and indicators of insufficient care and work with Tomas to develop a plan for response.
Elaine will reduce the number of stress-related symptoms that she experiences as a result of worrying about her school and work, by April 2003.	Elaine will explore with her counselor the history of stress in her life. Elaine will participate in a stress and burnout workshop. Elaine will not work on the weekends or before 6:00 a.m. or past 6:00 p.m. on work days.
Geoff will establish a friendship with one person, by May 2002. Geoff will report that he has a friend that he cares about, enjoys being with, and knows cares about him, by October 2002.	Geoff's worker will meet with him on a regular basis, once a week, to discuss relationships, and his skills for making and being in relationship. Geoff's worker will accompany him to recreational volleyball at the community centre on Tuesday nights, and they will stay for juice and cookies after the practices and games.
Pam will identify the ways that she would like to pursue and express her interest in spirituality, by March 2002.	Pam will join a group that discusses the nature of spirituality. Pam will find a course on spirituality and take it. Pam and her mother will go to a weekend meditation retreat. Pam will read books on spirituality.
The Milne family members will be able to discuss and explain different ways of thinking about addiction, by September 2004.	The family worker will convene a family meeting and assist the family members in speaking with each other about the addiction and its impact. The family worker will find a suitable course on addictions for this family and recommend it to the family.
Family members will be able to discuss Mom without family incidents and reactions, by June 2003.	Mr. Macintosh will attend sessions with a grief counselor. The family counselor will hold sessions with this family that allow for talking about Mom and will assist them in redefining the family without Mom.
The Singh family will feel less shame about having a child with a disability, by October 2004.	The special needs worker will arrange for two other families of similar cultural background and who have children with autism to call them. The worker will take them to a "Parents of a Disabled Child" meeting.
Emily and Brian will accept that the other members of their family want to continue in the church, by January 2003.	The family worker will meet with Emily and Brian together to assist them in coming to terms with their family members' choice to continue with the church. The family worker will meet with the other family members as well and eventually bring the two groups together in order to resolve their differences.

Continued

Table 5.5. Examples of Service Actions

Goal Statement Examples	Service Action Examples
The group will identify the strengths, weaknesses, and capacities of the members of collective, by June 2003.	A facilitator will meet with the group for one day to identify strengths, weaknesses, and capacities.
An equity policy and a plan for promoting equality of rights and anti-discrimination will be developed by the gay/lesbian/bisexual community in collaboration with other marginalized groups, by December 2003.	The group will meet with the equity adviser and other selected groups over the next six months to develop a shared policy. The group will meet with a facilitator to create a working group to change things within the organization with regard to acceptance of sexual minority members of the community.
A new recruitment strategy, aimed at engaging practitioners who are creative, open-minded, and energetic, will be put in place, by September 2003.	A facilitator will assist the team in brainstorming ideas about different ways to recruit the kind of people that they are seeking. The facilitator will continue to work with the organization until they have a vision and plan in place. The facilitator will train the team in learning organization theory, and will get them to identify what they need and want to learn about in order to bring about a more functioning organization. The facilitator will provide or find the necessary training.

Table 5.5. *Continued*

Service Action Example	
Geoff's worker will accompany him to recreational volleyball at the community centre on Tuesday nights, and they will stay for juice and cookies after the practices and games.	Overall Service Action: Geoff will establish one friendship with one person, by May 2003.
	Sessional Service Action: At the first Tuesday evening volleyball practice, Geoff's worker will introduce Geoff to the coordinator and engage Geoff and the coordinator in a conversation. The worker will model for Geoff how he might say hello and introduce himself to others. At any sign that Geoff is willing to move around the room during the juice break and make eye contact with others, the worker will acknowledge his efforts.

Table 5.6. Examples of Overall and Sessional Service Action Statements

would do and whether we achieved the desired outcome, results, or happy ending wanted by the client. Evaluation gives the practitioner a reading on how the client is progressing and how the practitioner is performing.

Only by systematically collecting information about the case as it unfolds can a practitioner know whether it is going as planned; anything less is speculation, professional guessing, an opinion, or a good hunch. In effect, the evaluation data is the feedback to the planning process. Although sometimes it seems advantageous to not know what is going on—this allows practitioners to think and do what they want—it is contrary to the purpose of planning. Evaluation indicates whether the case is going according to plan; if it is not, a new, more appropriate and more effective plan can be developed.

> Only by systematically collecting information about the case as it unfolds can a practitioner know whether it is going as planned; anything less is speculation, professional guessing, an opinion, or a good hunch.

The importance of case evaluation is represented by the fact that it is one of the four constructs in the model of planned change/case plan formulation. Clearly, it is not an afterthought or just something to be done if or when there is time. Because it is viewed as a key construct, not to engage in case evaluation would mean not to engage in planning.

Evaluation in our model involves addressing the following questions and having a plan that answers these four questions:

1. What do I want to know about this case?
2. What information would I take as evidence of knowing?
3. How would I use the information?
4. How will I collect what I want to know?

To address the question, "What do I want to know about this case?", there are four evaluation questions that are inherent in the model:

1. Did the troublesome behavior(s) go away? (Was it replaced by appropriate or inappropriate alternatives?)
2. Were the need(s) met?
3. Were the goal(s) met?
4. Did we do what we said we would do in terms of service action? Did we do it consistently?

These questions are obvious and can be answered by straightforward monitoring of descriptive information. Other questions are less obvious and more complex:

- The client(s) profile—who did we see?
- Did the service action account for either the troublesome behavior going away, the need being met, or the goal being met?
- Did different service actions get used for different clients?
- Were some clients more likely than others to reach their goals?
- Was the goal a success because of what we did or was it a function of the nature of the clients? Or both?

In the case of the Macintosh/Jones family, the need was for each member of the family to grieve in her or his own way over the loss of Mom and rethink how the family will be now that she is gone. One of the goals is for Mr. Macintosh to allow other family members to talk about Mom in his presence. The service action is for Mr. Macintosh to participate in grief counseling and participate in discussions about Mom while being guided by the counselor. Within the context of the grief counseling, the counselor will have sessional service action strategies. Theoretically, it could be argued that the evaluation question should cover everything; for example, did the troublesome behavior go away, did the need get met, did the goal get met, did we do what we said we would do? However, this kind of indiscriminate information demand results in both indiscriminate thinking and indiscriminate evaluation planning. Indiscriminate information demand usually has one of two outcomes:

1. Nothing collected
2. Everything collected and nothing used.

In other words, knowing what information needs exist is as critical as knowing what client needs exist. The information need is defined when the practitioner and the organization define what they can and will use.

To continue with the Macintosh/Jones family, assume that the practitioner wants to know whether Mr. Macintosh and his family reached their goals and whether this met their needs. The practitioner must then establish two things. First, how will the information be used? It could be used to determine whether to conclude the work with the family; however,

> **The practitioner must determine what will be taken as evidence.**

if the goal was reached but the need was not met, the information alerts the practitioner to reassess the situation to determine either a more relevant goal or more finely-tuned service actions.

The second thing the practitioner must do is determine what will be taken as evidence. Evidence of Mr. Macintosh allowing others to speak about Mom in his presence may be that when any family member talks about Mom, he stays in the room, or he doesn't interrupt to change the subject, or he participates in the conversation. The point is that what will be taken as evidence of the case being on track must be specified at the beginning of service action.

Once the practitioner knows what to know, clarifies how it will be used, and identifies what will be taken as evidence of it, then information-collection strategies and procedures and the length of time necessary for the collection of evidence can be established.

In summary, then, an evaluation plan addresses four things:

1. What we want to know
2. What is to be taken as evidence of knowing
3. How the information will be used
4. How the information is to be collected.

Summary

The planning process is fundamentally a way of thinking about our practice. Planning occurs within the broader context of practice. It comprises attending to and providing leadership for particular situations in which care is required. Planning is foremost a way of thinking about how to plan for change for those seeking care. No two cases will look alike. There will be different terms of assessment and case plan formulation (See Figure 5.7). There will be different kinds of goals that suit different cases. There will be different indicators of success used to determine whether there is goal success and consistency in the application of service. On the other hand, all cases will look alike in that every case is considered in terms of assessment and case plan formulation.

> Planning is foremost a way of thinking about how to plan for change for those seeking care. No two cases will look alike.

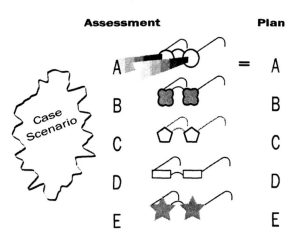

Figure 5.7.   No Two Cases Will Look Alike.

Integrated Case Planning Models

We have described assessment and case plan formulation as inquiry processes guided by frameworks that clarify intent and result in shared understanding about issues, needs, goals, service actions, and evaluation. We have suggested that the clients' perspective is critical to the inquiry process. They are the experts on their lives. We have also suggested that assessment and case plan formulations will be stronger and clearer when people who have an interest in or commitment to the client are involved in the inquiry and planning processes. In this section we propose ideas about how to create integrated or across agency planning models.

In these times many speak about the need to work together in practice. Reports, articles, and policies call for more integration, integrated case management, integrated service delivery, integrated practice, multidisciplinarity, interdisciplinarity, transdisciplinarity, collaboration, and collaborative practice. Such shifts in thinking and practicing are heralded as the "answer" to the challenges we face in our respective systems. While these intentions are good and the concepts are laudable, many of these terms have become part of the habitual language of our business without really conveying any meaning or significance that unites us in understanding. We have become anaesthetized to the potential underlying the terms.

Integration and, by association, integrated case planning fundamentally reflect a state of mind; a way of thinking that results in a way of acting in a collaborative way that enhances the capacity of people. When we work with others, we expand the perspectives on the issues, needs, and potential solutions and we bring to the table more resources and skills than any one of us can muster on our own. It is the only way to think and act (practice and plan) if we are to successfully confront our "messy problems"—those dynamic problems that are complex due to their interrelationships with other challenges and circumstances.

> Consider the life situation of a youth named Hector who lives in a small community somewhere in North America. Hector has been diagnosed with a mental illness as well

as a developmental disability attributed to Fetal Alcohol Syndrome. Hector's adoptive family is struggling to stay committed and connected to him. The family lives in a community where specialized resources are virtually non-existent and travel to a larger community 60 miles down the rough road is required to access most health care and social service resources. The community is also characterized by a high level of substance misuse, violence, and racial intolerance and Hector has begun to abuse solvents and is hanging out with a rough crowd. He has also been the victim of bullying and abuse at his school due to his mixed race heritage. How can any one person, or even agency, successfully meet the needs and goals for Hector and his family ... and why should they be expected to?

We believe that integrated case planning models can be developed and embedded within the day-to-day practice of our health and social service systems. One of the characteristics of models that are successful is that they have been co-created by the service providers working together within a community. There are some features of integrated case planning that are consistent across many different models and we offer these as a framework for consideration. They are:

- Principle and value based
- Inclusive of the people who are the focus of planning and others who have a role to play in the planning
- Intentional processes for planning.

Integrated Case Planning Principles and Values

Principles and values that are reflected in integrated case planning models include:

- Client-centred service: Clients are at the centre of all service planning and practice; the client's strengths as well as needs are identified and services are adapted to fit client needs.
- Holistic approach: Provides for a more complete understanding of the various aspects of a client's life context and needs, and the development of a case plan formulation that reflects this broader context.
- Inclusion and participation: The client, significant people in the client's life whom the client wishes to have involved and all the service providers who have a role to play in assessment, plan formulation, service action, and evaluation are engaged in the process and agree to participate as fully as possible.
- Building on strengths and building capacity: Specific solutions accommodate the strengths, capacities of people, and ways in which capacity can be enhanced for long-term well-being.
- Recognizing diversity: Integrated case planning models respect and respond to the social, cultural, and economic factors that shape clients' lives.
- Mutual respect: Participants show respect for one another's knowledge, skills, experience and perspective regardless of training, discipline, position, classification, agency affiliation, or history; they foster a climate of respect for clients.

- Accountability: Integrated case planning models are accountable to the people being served through the process and to the participants in the process. They are also accountable to the agencies and systems involved for the purposes of continuous learning and improvement as well as efficient and effective use of available resources. Models are thoughtful and intentional processes for assessment, planning, evaluation, and documentation.

Inclusion

Integrated case planning refers to a team approach taken to coordinate various services for a specific purpose, such as for an individual or family, through a cohesive and sensible plan. All members of the team work together to identify the issues, assess, formulate plans, take action, and evaluate and record developments and progress. One of the key characteristics of integrated case planning is that the client and the significant people in the client's life are involved in the process wherever possible. The team should also include all service providers who have a role in or contribution to make to the planning process. Integrated case planning goes beyond cooperation, coordination or even collaboration, although all of these are elements as well as outcomes of integrated case planning. Integrated case planning is about the various players co-creating a process that they commit to using when the people whom they serve have needs that cut across disciplines, agency mandates, and jurisdictions.

Intentionality

Integrated case planning models are thoughtful and intentional processes for assessment, planning, service action, evaluation, and documentation. As mentioned earlier, there is no one right way to do integrated case planning and there are a variety of models that may work well. Perhaps most important is that there is shared agreement amongst the parties to the process about how it will look. Key elements include:

- Shared principles and values that are well understood
- Development of trusting relationships
- Common goals
- Clear delineation of responsibilities
- Clarity about what information will be shared and with whom, with an emphasis upon open and honest communication
- Shared responsibility and accountability for the process and outcomes
- Mechanism for resolving conflicts

There are also particular techniques or actions that are typical of integrated case planning models, notably:

- Integrated case conferences
- Proactive assessment, planning, action, review and implementation
- Follow-through and follow-up with continuous reassessment
- Designation of a case coordinator
- Clarity about documentation and recording—what, where, who, and how?

Integrated Planning Beyond "The Case"

Because integrated planning and practice is fundamentally a way thinking and acting that is value and principle-based, it is applicable to planning and practice for individual cases, programs, policy development, training and education, and research and evaluation.

Any situation in which the players involved have the following realizations can benefit from an integrated approach:

- What we are doing isn't working
- The problem is greater than any one of us can meet on our own
- We are interdependent with other people and groups
- The benefits of integration (e.g., effectiveness, efficiency, survival, strategic advantage) outweigh the risks (e.g., loss of control or status, threat to ideology or theoretical orientation)
- Self-interests are linked to common interests

Therefore, the qualities of integrated planning in any context include:

- Seeing the bigger picture and the complex interrelationships of needs and strengths
- Recognizing that others have to be engaged to achieve better processes and outcomes for the people or communities served
- Valuing the diversity of skill and perspective
- Sharing a common purpose
- Being committed to and trusting of others
- Being willing to share the risks and rewards of partnership
- Being willing to think and act differently and learn together.

Mapping the Planning Process

One technique that we found useful as we struggled to make more evident our own planning processes was "mind mapping." Mind maps are visual representations of our thinking and choice making in the face of certain situations. They make more explicit what we do or want to do. The material presented throughout this section represents our effort to make more explicit what we have found to be important elements in a planning process. Our mind maps (see Figures 5.8 and 5.9) helped us identify what was important to us and are included for your consideration.

> Mind maps are visual representations of our thinking and choice making in the face of certain situations.

More important, however, we encourage you to develop your own mind map on planning. The key point in this entire book, and this section in particular, is not that you accept or adopt what we propose, but that you analyze and make explicit who you are as an emergent practitioner, what contexts influence your practice and how, what planning processes you use, and why and how you use them. You will have your own unique

> You have your own unique approaches for developing knowledge about yourself, obtaining understanding about the contexts for practice, and engaging in planning.

approaches for developing knowledge about yourself, obtaining understanding about the contexts for practice, and engaging in planning. Mind maps may help you make these approaches more explicit.

To give you an opportunity to create a mind map, we have included the following case for you to work through. As you consider the information and story of this case, notice where your mind goes in terms of what is important and what is not. Notice who you would have interviewed first, second, and third. What are the mistakes you think we made in our assumptions? What were your assumptions? Pay attention to what you do not know from the information presented and what other information you would like to have. Do you have a different formulation of the case? What information do you use to make the different formulation? What process do you use to think through the information? What process do you use to think through the formulation? What needs, goals, service actions, and evaluation ideas occurred to you? Then, draw your map.

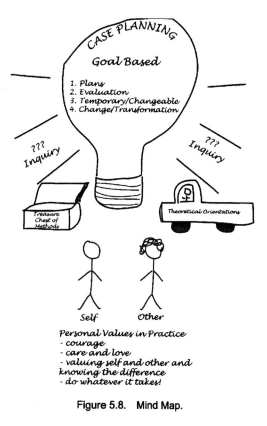

Figure 5.8.   Mind Map.

This case example represents a composite of situations that we have worked on in the past. We have created this composite in order to protect the confidentiality of all people involved, although the thoughts and actions recorded do represent our actual practice. The purpose of the example is to illustrate the following points:

- Continuous inquiry is the foundation for practice.
- Our practice is influenced by who we are as emergent practitioners and the contexts within which we work, both of which are inevitably complex.
- There is a process for practice that changes each time.
- Assessment is a critical and recurrent step within that process.
- In practice, we are concurrently moving in and out of—and cycling back and forth between—alerting, assessing, planning, acting, and evaluating. Sometimes we do this even between the breaths that we take.

I was a case worker responsible for finding and monitoring resources for the children in our care. Jason was a six-year-old boy in care. He was living in one of the resources that I had recently become responsible for, although I had not yet met him nor was I familiar with the resource. At one of our daily team meetings, in which new referrals and requests were reviewed and allocated to workers for follow-up, my supervisor asked me to look into Jason's situation. His new case worker had some concerns about the

Inquiry Process

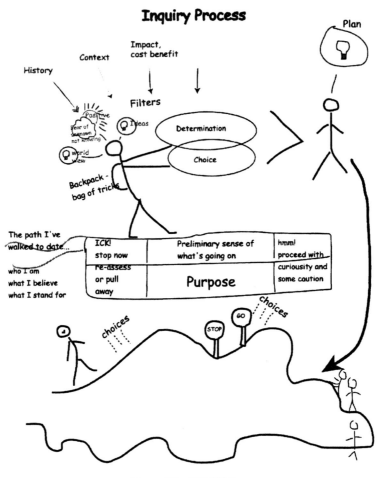

Figure 5.9. Mind Map.

suitability of his placement. Several of my colleagues offered bits of information about Jason and suggested that he was a hard child to place.

Back in my office I pulled the files that we held on the resource and Jason's placement. I had come to realize that these files rarely told much of the story, but for me they were a place to start. I was already questioning why a child of six had been placed in a large group-living resource that I knew was intended for older children. What was going on here? Was this working for Jason and his family?

The files told me bits of the story. Jason was in care at the request of, and through agreement with, his mother. She had apparently been unable to cope with his "extreme" behaviors and aggression towards his two younger siblings. Mom hoped that he could receive some treatment in care, and she needed a break. My mind was flooded with questions about Jason and his family. Had Jason been abused? By whom, how, for how long? Where was Dad and other members of the extended family? What was Mom like? Who was she connected to? How old were Jason's siblings? What had happened between Jason and his siblings? Was Jason in school or involved in the community in any way?

Who was involved in Jason's life, care, and treatment? What was working for him? What was not working for him? How would I know?

The file suggested that the criteria applied to the placement selection included bed availability, no younger children, availability of expressive therapies, and staff with experience in caring for children who have been sexually abused. Jason had been placed in a group home for older children and had been there for three months. Another host of questions emerged. How was Jason doing in the group home? Was he settling in and feeling safe there? What was it like for him to be with so many other children who were older? Was he in school? What did he like to do? Was he able to do it in the group home (particularly with so many older children)? What was the program for Jason? What was the group home's therapeutic philosophy? What was the plan of care? Who was involved in his care and treatment? How involved was Jason's case worker? Who knew Jason? Was the group home including the family in any aspect of his care?

The case of Jason took on a different level of significance for me. Things did not feel right to me already and the process of discovery had just begun. I was aware that I had a specific role to play in Jason's life and case. My job, as defined by the organization that employed me, was to find suitable placements for children in care, monitor the quality of care provided in these placements, and provide arms-length support to the placements as necessary. I was largely dependent upon the information and knowledge that others had about a child or youth. Although I was not prevented from doing direct "assessments" with the children and youth I was to place, I was also not encouraged to spend much time with them. In Jason's case, I had been asked to review the suitability of the placement with the worker. If need be, I would also be expected to find another placement for Jason.

Despite the restrictions placed on my practice, I decided to pay a visit to the group home and meet Jason. I arrived shortly after lunch. The other children had returned to school, staff were cleaning up in the kitchen, and Jason was sitting in the playroom watching television. I introduced myself and asked if I could sit down. He nodded approval and continued to watch television. As I sat on the couch several feet away from him, he bounced up, moved to the other side of the room, grabbed a large stuffed bear off the shelf, and pushed its nose in. Jason's eyes moved between me, the television, the bear, and the door. I sat quietly for awhile, pretending to watch the television. Jason moved closer to the television, then dropped the bear and sat on it. He pulled a bear leg up towards him and rocked back and forth while he tried to pull out the fuzz of the bear's coat.

Following a few more minutes of silence, I asked Jason if he liked the television program that he was watching. A shrug of the shoulders provided the response. I waited for a few moments, then asked whether he had seen the show before. This time I received a verbal response. Slowly and cautiously, I worked at engaging Jason. The number of words he spoke that day probably amounted to no more than 25; however, he did look at me several times and his rocking behavior subsided. I was observing closely and gathering information, although I had little idea at this point what its significance was. I felt challenged in his presence as his verbal skills were limited. How could I know what he was thinking and feeling? The questions kept coming in my mind: Who are you little Jason? What is happening for you? What do you need?

After an hour I said a casual goodbye to Jason and I retreated to the kitchen to speak with several staff. They shared little with me about Jason, other than that he was not getting along with the other children. The staff seemed anxious about speaking with me and suggested that it would be better to speak with the program supervisor when she became available. The questions kept coming. Why the anxiety and awkwardness?

What do they mean that he doesn't fit in here? What does that look like? How does this place run? I headed back to my office and was quickly engaged in other cases and issues, although half-conscious of the fact that I still felt none the wiser about Jason and his situation.

Some time later I called the caseworker. She too was new to Jason's case and had not yet met him, although she had met with the mother. She felt that it was inappropriate that Jason was in a group home with older children. She was concerned that he would be abused again. I asked what she meant. She seemed surprised at the question until I explained that the files that I had reviewed shared little about Jason and his family's situation. The worker stated that because Jason had been sexually abused she was concerned that he would be a mark in a group home full of older children and was more likely to re-experience abuse. She also said that she had heard the resource did not provide adequate supervision of the children and she had little confidence in the program. Her preference, she said, was for Jason to be placed in a foster home.

Our discussion continued and Jason's worker pulled her files and began to read excerpts for me. Jason's father sexually abused him and brought others into the home to do the same. His siblings had also been abused, although apparently to a lesser degree. The abuse started when they were very young and had continued until the father was charged with the abuse and jailed. The father was currently in jail. The family became involved with the authorities 18 months ago (when Jason was four) as a result of a report made by a physician who felt that there was unequivocal evidence of sexual abuse. Jason's mom knew that something terrible was happening to her children; however, she lived in fear of her life and had felt unable to take action. She claimed that she didn't know that they were being sexually abused. Initially all the children were removed from her care. Mom established a new home, reconnected with her supportive extended family, and successfully petitioned to have the children returned to her care. Mom was involved in individual counseling, a parenting program, and two self-help groups. The children were each involved in expressive therapies and Jason had been assigned a part-time behavioral support worker in the school. Jason had also been observed and interviewed at some length by a psychiatrist as part of the evidence gathering that was necessary to convict his father. Mom could not cope with Jason at this time in her life, however, and she asked that he be taken back into care and provided with more intensive treatment than what was available in the community.

I can recall feeling appalled that Jason had had to live through such horror. I reflected on the happy, playful, and competent six-year-olds that were such a vital part of my personal life at the time and I felt very sad. At the same time, I recall feeling ill-prepared to take any action on behalf of Jason. I felt that I was coming to know some things about him, but still had little understanding about who he was and what he needed. I had begun to formulate that Jason was a sexually-abused child, his development was delayed as a result of the trauma, he had little capacity for empathy, and his family has limited capacity to deal with him. I also had information on the current services being provided to Jason and his family. However, for every question that I had answered, several more emerged.

While Jason's worker was initially willing to discuss the case with me, she was reluctant to share the more complete case files and assessments. Instead, she preferred to interpret them for me. In retrospect, I realize that she had developed her own understanding and formulation about Jason and his family. She viewed me as being responsible for executing the plan that she had formulated. Despite this, she did give me the names and phone numbers of several people involved in Jason's life. I continued to gather information, although given the sensitivities and my role in the case, I was clear with everyone that my purpose was to understand Jason's needs so that the best possible living arrangement could be established for him.

I spoke with Jason's mom, her new partner, the psychiatrist, Jason's former teacher and principal, and the group-home supervisor. My questions focused on learning more about Jason and the people around him. What did Jason do well? What was difficult for him? How did he compare to other children his age? What did he do with other children? How did Mom describe Jason? What did she think he needed? What was the new boyfriend like? How were they managing the other children? What seemed to be her strengths and challenges? What did she want in the future? Did she have plans for getting there? How much time and energy did she have to be involved in Jason's life during his placement?

I visited Jason at different times of the day. We spoke occasionally, although most of what I learned came through my observations of Jason's behavior. I spoke with my supervisor and colleagues. Bit by bit I gathered, sifted, and sorted information. I alternated between thinking that I did understand Jason and his needs, and thinking that I still didn't have a clue. I frequently seized on the ideas and assessments of others and followed them up only to gather additional information that seemed to conflict with earlier assessments and formulations. Clearly, there were many different ways to look at Jason's situation.

I felt confident about my assessment that Jason had been severely traumatized by the actions of both parents. His father was his abuser, and his mother did not protect him. He needed very careful, skillful, and knowledgeable nurturing in order to trust adults. I was confident, although alone, in my assessment that the mother, while trying hard and demonstrating great strength as a survivor of abuse herself, was unlikely to ever be able to give Jason all that he needed in a sustained way. Nonetheless, it would be significant for Jason to have his mother consistently and positively involved in his life. I doubted that Jason would thrive in an environment with other children and felt that he needed to be an only child for a while.

I also believed that despite all the professional people who had been involved in Jason's life, a thorough assessment had still not been done. Further, due to the busy schedules of people involved with Jason, no case conference was ever organized. This presented an interesting challenge to me as a professional working within a broad and complex system of care. Should I raise my concerns about the lack of adequate assessment? If so, with whom and how? What was my responsibility as a practitioner to act, even though I had doubts about the comprehensiveness of my assessment?

I made a decision to act on the basis of what I had and began the process of assessing potential caregivers. New layers of assessment, planning, and evaluating were initiated as I sought to learn about different caregivers and assess their capacity in the context of Jason's needs. In the end I recruited caregivers that were not only highly skilled but also committed to developing a long-term relationship with Jason and his mom and siblings. At this point the nature of my work shifted, although I was still engaged in a continuous process of assessing, planning, and evaluating. We began to prepare Jason for the move from the group home to his new foster home. I spent many hours with the foster parents discussing what supports they might need to make the placement a success. We initiated visits and paid attention to Jason's readiness to move. Finally, Jason moved into his new home.

Once again, another layer of assessment, planning, and evaluating was added to the process as my role moved to that of supporting the foster parents and monitoring the quality of care. Indeed the process continued until I left for another job and someone else took up the role. Even then, many years later I heard from the foster parents. Jason lived with them for five years and eventually returned to live with his mother. Jason was surviving, although he still struggled with a number of issues. He regularly called and visited with the foster parents. His younger brother had also come into care and lived with the foster parents for a year. His behavior and needs proved to be even more challenging than Jason's, and after a year a decision was made to place him in a more intensive treatment program. The foster parents were exhausted and had decided to pursue other careers. I wondered what might have been different in this case had I continued to be involved, or had there been a different set of people involved in Jason's care. Would my views of Jason's mom have changed? Would I have identified concerns about Jason's brother? How would things have been different? I have no doubt that the case would have unfolded differently had I continued to be involved. Just as I am sure that had a different practitioner been involved in the first place, the decisions and plans made would be different. Just as I am sure that had I come to be involved in this case at this point in my career, my process and practice would look different. These differences do not represent a good or bad judgment on my part; they are just indicative of the emergent nature of practice.

Case Planning Systems

It is important not to confuse planning thinking with planning systems. Planning systems are formally organized and standardized procedures for conducting planning in practice. They serve to ensure equal access and care within a larger system and define case management or planning procedures and roles. They are discussed below, and examples are found in Appendix D. Practitioners who want to coordinate planning within and across agencies require a common model for conceptualizing planning and then a planning system based on that model. Having a shared and underlying philosophy of care makes the creation of the planning system more congruent.

The first requirement for setting up a planning system is to have frameworks or models for alerting, assessing, and formulating case plans. These frameworks or models specify how agency personnel are to think about each aspect of the planning process, which, in turn, points to the establishment of certain procedures. For example, if the case plan formulation model is the one presented earlier, one procedure will be goal setting, another will be deciding on a service plan, and another will be evaluating.

A second requirement is to know who is involved, what decisions are made, what gets documented, and when situations get identified (i.e., when we become alert to them), assessed, planned, and implemented. We do not intend to describe a complete planning system here because such systems work best when they are designed to meet the needs of particular institutions. However, in Appendix D, we offer you questions to consider as you engage in defining integrated case planning systems and procedures.

Case planning processes, as described above, may be defined within a case planning system. This agreed-upon approach to undertaking case planning may be personally defined, as when individual practitioners define what their system will be, or it may be organizationally defined. The key is that the process is made explicit.

One reason for having a planning system is to ensure that all cases have equal access and assured standards of care, no matter where they come from, who they are, or who knows them. Another reason is to ensure that all cases are moved through the system in a caring, efficient, and effective way. This is especially important in large systems that have many referrals, conduct many assessments, and generate many plans for children, youth, and families. When "what happens" is left to an individual practitioner's decision making, then standards of practice may be inconsistent at best, and unprofessional or unethical at worst. Systems are designed to "take care" of persons in the systems equally, while ensuring that individual concerns are heard and accommodated.

Planning systems reflect a set of values (see Appendices C and D) and must be thought through in terms of those values. The values are evidenced in the planning model as well as in the procedures for the case planning system. Some values might include deliberate care, efficiency, effective care, and thoughtful, voluntary practice, to mention a few. All planning systems benefit from being thought through in terms of their underlying philosophy, because it is the underlying philosophy that dictates how people are treated and managed. Not clarifying such philosophies may well result in a simple processing of people through the system, although simple processing can happen with or without a planning system. How one relates to people depends on one's values and not necessarily one's procedures.

We suggest that planning systems have the following elements:

- Statement of purpose and vision
- Statement of underlying beliefs and values
- Explicit outline of the planning process from alert through to follow-up
- Explicit outline of a model for planned change
- Identification of approaches to and mechanisms for monitoring, evaluation, and review.

(Examples are presented in Appendices C and D).

Conclusion

A conclusion implies that we are done. To be done with is "to be finished with," to "be over." Being done is antithetical to the ideas of inquiry, continuous learning, and emergence that are presented in this book. Just as emergent practice planning is easier said than done, thoughtful closure is easier said than done.

It is our intention to be thoughtful in creating a conclusion that will continue to engage you in ongoing learning and emergence. The book is done but you are not. Your emergent practice planning journey continues.

The questions posed create an opportunity for you to take stock of where you have been, where you are now, and where you want to go next. Notice what you think you know. Notice what you thought you knew but now know that you didn't know. Notice the questions that are unanswered as well as those that are emerging in this intentional process of inquiry in practice and practice planning. The questions are framed in terms of the EPP framework.

When you consider the process of being engaged in making intentional choices and discretionary judgments:

- Do you act intentionally in practice, and if not, how do you explain that you do not?
- What is your assessment of your capacity to exercise discretion in your practice?
- What fetters your discretion?
- How will you enhance your capacity and opportunity to make choices and discretionary judgments?

When you consider Self as Practitioner:

- What importance do you attach to having the right answers?
- What are the fundamental beliefs and values that define your practice and practice planning?

- What is your theoretical orientation?
- What language do you use to describe those you work with, who you work for, and what you do?
- What is your process for staying in inquiry?
- How will you enhance your capacity to be "present" with clients, with colleagues, and within your work system?

When you consider the Context of Practice:

- What are the contexts that you experience in practice?
- What is your attitude toward complexity of contexts and has it shifted as you worked through this book?
- How do you work with the expectations of multiple contexts in your practice?
- When do you give up with complexity and what do you do when you "give up"?
- How will you enhance your capacity to embrace complexity in practice and practice planning?

When you consider Practice Planning (models and frameworks):

- What are the dominant models in use around you in your practice?
- What models do you use and do these models serve effective practice and practice planning?
- What keeps you from changing to models that would be more effective?
- Do you have your own processes for "alert, assess, plan, and act"?
- What intrudes on your processes for these functions and how do you handle the intrusion?
- What new or different models and frameworks would enhance your practice and practice planning?
- Will you be taking any models and frameworks from this book to integrate into your practice and practice planning?

As you considered these questions:

- Which questions made you uncomfortable?
- Which questions did you skip over because they were too hard?
- Which questions did you joke about and toss off lightly?
- Which questions brought "real" situations to mind and triggered emotions? What were the emotions?
- How are these emotions related to your beliefs and values about practice and practice planning?
- Which questions did you respond to in a more thoughtful way as a result of learning EPP?
- Were you able to give yourself permission to struggle and not know?

The reflection that you engaged in while answering these questions is the kind of reflection required in practice for new learning and personal change. To stay in inquiry in practice we suggest that **nothing is conclusive**. Allow this idea to assist you in maintaining an iterative process of reflection, assessment, and creation.

Appendix A: Context Models

Self-Driven Ethical Decision-Making Model

In their self-driven model, Garfat and Ricks (1995) discuss the context for ethical practice. They point out that self-driven ethical decisions are informed by the person making the decision, by factors in the situation, and by a process of critical and reflective analysis within the current context. Their model makes explicit a number of contextual factors that affect or impinge on the decision-making process, including the practitioner's personal framework for ethical decision making; professional codes of ethics and standards of practice that are confronted, evaluated, and actualized through the self and applied to the situation; and the process of problem solving or decision making for ethical practice issues (see Figure A.1). Following the decision, any action taken is evaluated and provides feedback to the problem-solving process and to the practitioner's framework, which is validated or modified in order to respond to future situations.

A key aspect of this model is the premise that ethical practice, including the resolution to the dilemma, is driven by the self. Self and the practice of ethics are interactively linked to the point of being inseparable. Therefore, the awareness and use of self are primary components within an ethical practice context.

There are implications in using this model. The first implication is the need to know oneself. Practitioners must know their experiences and their beliefs and values, and how those beliefs and values act upon the self, others, and the context, in the moment. Only by being self-aware does one distinguish oneself from the others; being able to make this distinction is critical for ethical practice. Self-awareness is practical because it challenges how we think about our practice, including our basic premises of practice. It requires a practical knowledge of what we think, how we feel, and what we do in particular situations and how those thoughts, feelings, and actions are grounded in strongly held beliefs and values.

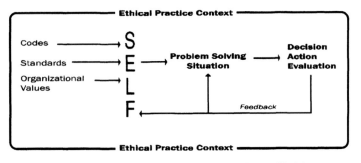

Figure A.1.   Self-Driven Ethical Decision-Making Model.

A second implication is the need for the practitioner to understand and take personal responsibility for ethical decision making. Doing so, however, involves more than acknowledging the responsibility. It involves a commitment to decide on, and follow through with, any necessary action. True responsibility requires that practitioners take whatever actions are necessary for the ethical analysis to become the ethical reality.

A third implication is that the practitioner needs to generate multiple alternatives. We are limited by those alternatives within our reality. Generating alternatives different from those within our reality requires the capacity to reach outside of our personal paradigm, suspending our beliefs about what is right or wrong, or about what is going to work or not. This is linked again to self-awareness as one considers questions such as: What if I did not believe ...? What if I did not value ...? What if I believed that ...? What if I valued ...? Generating alternatives outside the box requires getting out of the box and taking a different perspective.

Finally, the practitioner needs a decision-making process informed by an evaluation and feedback mechanism. Evaluation is the systematic collection of data for decision making and planning. The capacity to collect and reflect on information in light of personal awareness of beliefs and values is a complex reflective process. There is little or no downtime in the practice situation! Practitioners are always monitoring information, considering it in light of their beliefs and values, and then generating their own meaning (usually based on meaning attributed by the client) in order to make a decision. The process depends on us identifying and challenging assumptions that underlie our ideas, values, beliefs, and actions; challenging the role and importance of context in influencing our thoughts and actions; imagining and exploring alternatives to existing ways of thinking and living; and engaging in relative skepticism.

A Social System Model

This model offers a way to understand a family, a community, or an organization by exploring how subsystems function within the larger system. The social systems approach explores functional relationships of structural components that exist in a social system. Most models consider the operating system in terms of the following structural components: input, functions, output, feedback mechanisms, and controls (see Figure A.2).

Input refers to the resources that sustain the system, such as money, people, or hard assets. Functions are the activities that the system carries out in order to conduct operations, or everyday business. Output refers to the result or production of the system that is acceptable to the

Controls		
(rules, regulations, laws, policy, values)		
Input	Functions	Output
(resources)	(activities)	(satisfaction, written record and memory)
Feedback		

Figure A.2.   A Social System Model.

Controls		
Once married, always married (family rule)		
Both parents care for household and children (family rule)		
Family Relations Act (legislation)		
Child and Family Services Act (legislation)		
Children are a cherished resource that belong to the community (community value)		
Input	Functions	Output
Wife/Mom Husband/Dad	Take care of household Parenting	Clean house and satisfaction Healthy kids
Three Children		
Grandparents	Grandparenting	Happy kids and satisfied parents
Two Incomes	Working at jobs	Money, satisfaction
Feedback		
Stay together, keep working, buy new house		

Figure A.3.   A Social System Model Applied.

same or other systems. Feedback mechanisms are the system's need satisfaction, written records, and memory. Controls are the rules, regulations, laws, values, or policy that constrain or impinge on the social system and affect what it can or cannot do, or how it can do what it does.

Figure A.3 shows how this model can be applied to a family and illustrates how the model organizes the practitioner's thinking.

Some practitioners have difficulty with social system models because they experience them as mechanistic and are unable to capture the affective components of the system. However, it is just a framework for thinking that allows practitioners to organize information collection for effective decision making and planning. Frameworks cannot keep you from being affective in practice!

The Ecological Model

The Ecological Model (Bronfenbrenner, 1979) is a complex model that defines different levels and aspects of context or environment. The premise of this model is that human development is a product of interaction between the growing individual and its evolving environment. What is important about this model is the premise that nothing is static. It focuses the practitioner on capturing aspects of the changing reality of the client, including the client's developmental changes. The model identifies some definitions and assumptions that are useful in assessing the client's environment.

The first definition speaks to the issue of how the growing individual is influenced by the environment.

> The ecology of human development involves the scientific study of the progressive, mutual accommodation between an active, growing human being and the changing properties of the immediate settings in which the developing person lives, as this process is affected by relations between these settings, and by the larger contexts in which the settings are embedded. (Bronfenbrenner, 1979, p. 21)

This definition presents a number of assumptions worth noting. First, the person and the environment influence each other. Second, the environment is conceived of as concentric structures or systems that are referred to as micro, meso, exo, and macro.

The microsystem is "a pattern of activities and roles and interpersonal relations experienced by the developing person in a given setting with particular physical and material characteristics" (p. 22). Settings include day cares, playgrounds, schools, churches, and so on. It is important for the practitioner to pay attention to the experience of the individual in the microsystem.

The mesosystem comprises "the interrelations among two or more settings in which the developing person actively participates" (p. 25). This might include the interrelations among home, school, peer group, and so on. An exosystem refers to "one or more settings that do not involve the developing person as an active agent, but in which events occur that affect, or are affected by, what happens in the setting of the developing person" (p. 25). For example, an exosystem might be each parent's work setting. The macrosystem refers to "consistencies, in the form and content of lower-order systems (micro, meso, and exo) that exist at the level of the subculture or the culture as a whole, along with any belief systems or ideology underlying such consistencies" (p. 26). Attitudes, legislation, policy, or shared values that represent a cultural position, such as "all children are entitled to and will be ensured an education," would represent a macrosystem. Another might be that "status and privilege make a difference in whether children attend school." An ecological transition occurs whenever a person's position in the ecological environment is altered as the result of a change in role or setting. When someone takes on a new job, or a woman becomes a mother, or when a close relative moves into the family home—these all represent ecological transitions.

These terms offer a framework for thinking about the individual within his or her context. One could create a mind map for thinking about the aspects of a person's world and how those aspects may be affecting the person and the issues being brought forward. For example:

- Micro: What are the person's interacting relations in different settings?
- Meso: What settings does this person participate in actively?
- Exo: What other settings affect this person's life, albeit indirectly?
- Macro: What are the ideological beliefs, rules, policies, and values that are present in this situation?
- Ecological transitions: What's happening that makes "change demands" on role, on setting, or on both?

Appendix B: Frameworks for Assessment

In gathering information about the problem, workers usually have frameworks that are used to collect and organize the information. Following are examples, not meant to be all inclusive, of different frameworks for data collection.

A Problem Framework

- Who is involved?
- How are participants involved?
- What meaning does the client ascribe to the problem?
- Where does the problematic behavior occur?
- When does the problematic behavior occur?
- What is the frequency of the problematic behavior?
- What is the duration of the problem?
- What unmet needs or wants are involved in the problem?
- What is the client's emotional reaction to the problem?
- How has the client attempted to cope with the problem, and what skills are required to solve it?
- What are the skills or strengths of the client related to the problem?

Or Personal Characteristics Framework

- Biophysical
- Physical

- Physical Health
- Cognitive/Intellectual
- Judgment
- Coherence
- Values
- Self-concept
- Emotional/Psychological

Or Context Characteristics Framework

- What is the individual functioning capability of the client(s), including their use of several key interpersonal subsystems?
- What is the motivation of the client(s) to work on specified target problems?
- Are there cultural problems embodied in the problem system, such as cultural norms and language?
- What are the interpersonal and communication dynamics involved in the spousal and family systems?
- Are there environmental factors that impinge upon the participants in the problem systems, such as social support?

These are only examples of frameworks for information. There are many others that may be applied within sessions, across sessions or for more holistic comprehensive case plan development.

Appendix C: Agency X Case-Planning System Policy Statement

To ensure efficient and effective case service at *X Child and Family Services*, the central office determines general policies and a generic model for case planning. Local areas utilize these policies and procedures. Regional policies and procedures are negotiated, reviewed, and approved by central office line management.

General Policy

A standardized case planning system guides and directs all assessment and treatment activities from referral to discharge. The case planning system incorporates the constructs and implied functions of Accountability Case Management, which include:

1. Constructs
   - Needs
   - Treatment Goals
   - Service Actions
   - Planning Evaluation
2. Functions
   - Assessment
   - Goal Setting
   - Service Planning/Intervention
   - Systematic Data Collection

This agency values case decision making that is based on assessment and treatment information; all case information that is collected and maintained addresses case planning.

Referral	Intake	Assessment Upon Admission to Service	Treatment Upon Completion of Needs Assessment	Review/Discharge	Service Section Planning
Who:					
Regional Designate	Regional Designate	Interdisciplinary team and selected others on demand as region designates	Interdisciplinary team and selected others on demand as region designates	Interdisciplinary team and selected others on demand as region designates	Regional service section designate take overall needs and goals and breaks down goals into short-term goals and service actions for next review period (specific indicators and data)
Decisions:					
Screen In Or Screen Out	Screen In Or Screen Out	Crisis Intake or Intake (a) priorize (b) assign for assessment (c) assessment questions (d) start date, set conference date (e) case coordinator	• Overall Needs • Overall Goals • Overall Services • Actions and Evaluation Criteria	• Progress on Overall Needs/Goals • Revised Overall Needs/Goals	Determine goals and service actions

Documentation:					
Regional Discretion (a) Release of information form 14	Regional Discretion (a) Release of information form 14	Includes: (a) Admission to Service form (b) Authorization for Service form (c) Completion of Consents for Release of Information (d) Intake data (e) Specified Service Areas (f) Assessment/assessment questions	Includes: (a) Relevant assessment reports (b) Conference summary (see policy)	Includes: (a) Additional assessment reports (b) Conference summary (see policy)	Regional Discussion
Procedures:					
Regional Discretion	Regional Discretion	Regional Discretion Program Director Directors represented by designate	Regional Discretion	Regional Discretion	Regional Discretion

Table C.1.　Case Management Functions

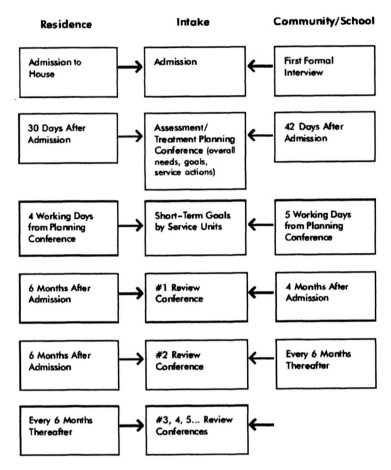

Figure C.1.   Case Conferencing.

Case planning incorporates an interdisciplinary treatment philosophy, with all disciplines adhering to existing case management policies and procedures.

Case planning documentation adheres to government regulations. Further documentation reflects the Accountability Case Management constructs: needs, treatment goals, service actions, and evaluation. Complete case files on current clients are maintained in the local offices.

Case planning system conferencing and file documentation are monitored twice a year by central office. Client case file documentation includes initial referral inquiry form; admission, transfer, and discharge forms; special-needs agreement for residential treatment and progress report authorizations; authorization for services (which includes medical consent); child history questionnaire; initial psychiatric, psychological, family, and residential assessment reports; previous agency reports; intake and treatment review conference summaries; extraordinary reports; and discharge summary.

Case planning occurs through systematic case conferencing at intake, assessment, treatment, and discharge. Service unit meetings ensure case planning that determines how service units assist client(s) in achieving treatment goals. Case coordinators are appointed to ensure that case plans are in place and proceeding as planned.

Obviously, this particular policy indicates the need for other definitions and procedures—for example, definition of case coordinator and job description for same, case planning audit procedures, and so on. It is not our intention to describe a complete case planning system here because case planning systems work best when they are designed to meet the needs of particular institutions. However, Table C.1 complements the written policy of agency X; it specifies the nature of each conference, who is present, the decisions to be made at each conference, and the appropriate documentation. Its purpose is to distinguish between having a conceptual framework for case planning and having policy and procedures for how to conduct case planning.

To understand more clearly the difference between policy and procedure, see Figure C.1. Figure C.1 identifies the conferences, and in some instances meetings, to be held for every case on a scheduled basis. This conference or meeting schedule is an example of a defined procedure that ensures the implementation of the policy statement, in this case policy #7. Only by developing these kinds of grids and schedules (as shown in Figure C.1) can practitioners cooperate, and subsequently coordinate, on case management. Put another way, to coordinate case management requires a case management system that specifically outlines who does what, when it is to be done, the decisions to be made at specific decision points, and how the case is documented.

In summary, case management occurs in a context of case practice. While individual practitioners may have their own case management procedures, standardized, efficient, and effective case management can only occur when there is a defined and articulated case management system. Case management systems are created within particular institutions or service delivery systems. To create a case management system requires the following steps:

1. Select a planned change model (e.g., Accountability Case Management)
2. Define case management policies
3. Define schedules and procedures based on a planned-change model and policies
4. Monitor/audit the system, revising if necessary

Appendix D: Integrated Case-Planning Policy and Practice

Jurisdictions throughout the developed world are experimenting with different approaches to integrated or collaborative case planning in health and social services. As discussed in Chapter 5, integrated case planning is fundamentally a state of mind and being—a way of thinking that results in a way of acting. In this appendix we present a policy and practice framework for integrated planning that you may adapt or recreate within your context.

Policy Framework

Increasingly, health and social service agencies are incorporating statements into their policies that speak to the importance of collaborating with other agencies or disciplines to develop an integrated plan of care or service for the people whom the agency serves. For example:

- The purpose of integrated case planning is to achieve better outcomes for the people we collectively serve.
- Integrated case planning is guided by the principles of inclusion, collaboration, mutual respect, and accountability.
- Integrated case planning requires service providers to identify and involve in the planning process the client(s), other professionals, community services, extended family, friends, and significant others in the client's life.
- Integrated case planning requires a documented plan that is signed off by all members of the team.
- Integrated case planning requires that there be one plan and one person designated as the case coordinator for the purposes of bringing together the people and other information necessary for effective planning and case progress.

- Integrated case planning requires each person on the team to participate in the assessment, planning, implementation, monitoring, and evaluation of the service plan. There will be a process to review the plan on a regular basis or whenever any member of the team, including the client, believes that the plan is no longer appropriate or adequate given the client's needs or goals. Conflicts that will arise during integrated case planning are resolved within the team.
- Integrated case planning provides a process to review the plan and its implementation where the needs of the client(s) exceed the capacity of the service providers or resources available.

In addition, policies show up that relate to or impact upon the capacity of practitioners to engage in collaborative planning and practice. These policies speak to information sharing and confidentiality (e.g., what information may be shared with whom and under what circumstances), working within agency mandate and resources available (e.g., what may be offered, what may not), and the "rules" for participation with other agencies and practitioners. Given the multiplicity of policies and rules that may influence the way in which we practice, it is important and helpful to remind ourselves of the principles of discretionary authority. Policies are guidelines or frameworks and are open to interpretation.

Conditions that Support Integrated Case Planning

Policies set the stage for integrated case planning but do not ensure that it is carried out or done well. Other factors help to create the conditions under which policy comes to life in practice. These include:

- Organizational factors: Practitioners are more likely to work in an integrated way if their own work context values and rewards innovation more than adherence to prescriptive organizational rules and regulations.
- Cultural factors: Within and between agencies and practitioners there are congruent visions, beliefs, values, and ethics that support collaboration, inclusion, openness and trust, continuous and mutual learning, and shared responsibility.
- Technical factors: Rules and procedures for working together are agreed upon; time and opportunity to work together is available; technical and administrative supports are provided to organize, facilitate, and record meetings; information systems are reliable and effective; practitioners have discretionary authority; and skilled and effective supervision is made available.
- Structural factors: Mechanisms or structures—such as joint team meetings, family conferences, and case conferences—exist to bring people together for planning; these include the people most affected by the plans.

Beginning Integrated Case Planning

Integrated case planning allows people to combine their knowledge and skills to produce an outcome that could not be achieved as effectively or efficiently through other means. As you contemplate your own capacity for and commitment to integrated case planning, key questions to ask yourself include:

- What are your criteria for initiating integrated case planning? What would be the indicators to you that integrated case planning would be of value for the client?
- What factors would influence your decision (e.g., your personal values and beliefs, experience with integrated approaches, familiarity with the other practitioners that would be involved, time available, your perspective on the complexity of the client's situation, organizational policies, etc.)?
- Who would need to be involved in the decision to initiate integrated case planning?
- What is your role in initiating integrated case planning?

Preparing for Integrated Case Planning

When a decision is made to initiate integrated case planning, it is helpful to make more explicit the terms and conditions that will guide the integrated case planning process. Key questions that may need to be considered include:

- What are the steps in preparing for an integrated case planning process (e.g., agreeing on need and purpose, deciding who to invite, agreeing on what approaches will be used to bring people together)?
- Who should be included? How will they be invited and prepared?
- What responsibilities would the client and significant others in the client's life have in integrated case planning?
- Is the client able to participate in the process? What would be necessary to support their inclusion? Who can provide assistance?
- What would be the responsibilities for the initiator, coordinator, facilitator, recorder, and other participants?
- What strategies or approaches will be used to bring people together for integrated case planning (e.g., family conference, case conference)?
- When will this happen? Who will arrange it and how will it be arranged?
- What is the role of supervisors and managers in supporting, guiding, or reviewing integrated case management?
- How will communication be ensured between practitioners and clients?
- How will differences of opinion and conflict be handled and resolved?

Integrated Assessment

Assessment is critically important to the planning process. Key questions to consider when approaching assessment through an integrated approach include:

- Who is able to contribute to the assessment?
- Are there any rules that will restrict information sharing? What can be done to overcome these barriers?

- What are the theoretical orientations and models of care that are represented within the integrated case planning team? What can be done to draw upon these differences to create a more holistic assessment?

Case Conferencing

Case conferencing is an approach or strategy that is commonly used to support integrated case planning. It creates the opportunity for people to physically come together and meet each other, and learn about the different perspectives that people have about a case situation as well as what each practitioner or agency might be able to offer in the development and implementation of the plan. Case conferences must be carefully organized and facilitated so that all participants are able to contribute to the discussions.

Follow-up and Closure

Integrated case planning is never truly "done"; it is in the process of getting there. The premise of integrated case planning is that positive outcomes will arise due to the integrated approach to planning—this implies that things will change. Change in a client's needs and circumstances must be understood in order to determine what shifts in planning are required. This cyclical process of assessment, action, and reflection requires that all participants in the integrated case planning process continue to engage with each other. To assist in managing follow-up, key questions for the integrated case planning participants to consider include:

- How will we know the plan is working?
- How will we monitor progress on agreed-upon goals?
- What circumstances or timeframes will indicate to us that we should reconvene for assessment and planning?
- Who will make this determination?
- How will information be shared between us over time and in between the formally arranged conferences?
- Are there new people who should be invited to participate?

Even when agencies or practitioners make a decision to close a file on a particular case, the chances are that someone within the integrated case planning context will continue to have some responsibility with the client. Key questions for the integrated case planning team to consider around closure include:

- How will decisions be made to "conclude" integrated case planning?
- How will the client be involved in that decision?
- Who will monitor and follow up after the conclusion of the integrated planning process?

Practitioners and agencies involved in integrated case planning are never "done" when determining how to be effective and efficient. They are always in a process of assessment, action, and reflection. It is particularly beneficial if participants set aside time to take stock of how the process is working or not working, and what could be done to make it work better for all concerned.

> As much as the consequences of failure [of collaboration] are far-reaching, the prizes are great. But the prizes do not go to the paperwork and the rhetoric but to the persistent, skillful, thoughtful, creative and committed who keep before them that it is vulnerable children who suffer most when the adults around them cannot or will not cooperate. (Morrison, 2002)

References

Adams, P., & Nelson, K. (1995). *Reinventing human services: Community and family-centered practice.* New York: Aldine De Gruyter.

Agathonos-Georgopoulou, H. (1998). Future outlook for child protection policies in Europe. *Child Abuse & Neglect, 22*(4), 239–247.

Allen-Meares, P. (1996, September 5). The new federal role in education and family services: Goal setting without responsibility. *Social Work, 41,* 533–540.

Argyris, C., & Schon, D. (1974). *Theory in practice: Increasing professional effectiveness.* San Francisco: Jossey-Bass Publishers.

Austin, C.D. (1990, September). Case management: Myths and realities. *Families in Society: The Journal of Contemporary Human Services, 71*(7) 398–407.

Austin, C.D. (1993, October). Case management: A systems perspective. *Families in Society: The Journal of Contemporary Human Services, 74*(8) 451–458.

Bateson, G. (1972). *Steps to an ecology of mind.* San Francisco: Author.

Bigelow, D.A., & Young, D.J. (1991, April 2). Effectiveness of a case management program. *Community Mental Health Journal, 27,* 115–123.

Bleakley, A. (1999). From reflective practice to holistic reflexivity. *Studies in Higher Education, 24*(3), 315–331.

Brissett-Chapman, S. (1997, January/February 1). Child protection risk assessment and African American children: Cultural ramifications for families and communities. *Child Welfare, LXXVI,* 45–63.

Brock, T., & Harknett, K. (1998, December). A comparison of two welfare-to-work case management models. *Social Service Review, 72*(4) 493–520.

Bronfenbrenner, U. (1979). *The ecology of human development: Experiments by nature and design.* Cambridge, MA: Harvard University Press.

Buzan, T. (1993). *The mind map.* London: BBC Books Enterprises Ltd.

Casto, M., & Julia, M.C. (1994). *Interprofessional care and collaborative practice.* Pacific Grove, CA: Brooks/Cole Publishing Company.

Christensen, D.N., & Todahl, J.L. (1999). Solution based casework: Case planning to reduce risk. *Journal of Family Social Work, 3*(4), 3–24.

Corcoran, J. (1998, October 4). Solution-focused practice with middle and high school at-risk youth. *Social Work in Education, 20,* 232–243.

Corey, G. (2001). *Theory and practice of counseling and psychotherapy* (6th ed.). Stamford, CT: Brooks/Cole Publishing.

Cottone, R.R. (1991, May/June). Counselor roles according to two counseling worldviews. *Journal of Counseling & Development, 69*, 398–401.

Elder, G.J. (1997). *The life course as developmental theory.* Washington, D.C.: University of North Carolina at Chapel Hill.

Elsdon, I. (1998). Educating toward awareness: Self-awareness in ethical decision-making for child and youth care workers. *Journal of Child and Youth Care, 12*(3), 55–67.

Farrell, T. (2001). Tailoring reflection to individual needs: A TESOL case study. *Journal of Education for Teaching, 27*(1), 23–39.

Freire, P., & Faundez, A. (1992). *Learning to question: A pedagogy of liberation.* New York: The Continuum Publishing Company.

Funk, A., & Kubo, R. (1996). *A checklist to guide the planning, development, implementation and review of partnership programs for children and youth.* Report prepared for the Vancouver Regional Child and Youth Committee. Vancouver, BC, Canada.

Garfat, T., & Ricks, F. (1995). Self-driven ethical decision-making: A model for child and youth care. *Child and Youth Care Forum, 24*(6), 393–403.

Garner, L. (1998). *The concept of discretionary authority in determining eligibility for welfare assistance.* Unpublished Master's thesis, Simon Fraser University, Vancouver, BC, Canada.

Hannigan, B. (2001). A discussion of strengths and weaknesses of 'reflection' in nursing practice and education. *Journal of Clinical Nursing, 10*(2), 278–284.

Hargreaves, A. (1996). Transforming knowledge: Blurring the boundaries between research, policy and practice. *Educational Evaluation and Policy Analysis, 18*(2), 105–122.

Hood, E., & Anglin, J. (1979). Chapter 4: The process of assessment. *Clinical Assessment in Children's Services.* Ottawa, ON: Children's Services Div., Ministry of Community and Social Services.

Howard, G. (1986). The scientist-practitioner in counseling psychology: Toward a deeper integration of theory, research, and practice. *The Counseling Psychologist, 14*(1), 61–105.

Hord, P. (1986). A synthesis of research on organizational collaboration. *Educational Leadership, 43*(5), 22–26.

Hurrell, P. (1996). *An International Inventory of "Best Practice" in Integrated Services Provision.* Report submitted to the Transition Commissioner for Child and Youth Services, Victoria, BC, Canada.

Isaacs, W.N. (1993). Taking flight: Dialogue, collective thinking, and organizational learning. *Organizational Dynamics*, Autumn, 24–39.

Korbin, J.E., & Coulton, C.J. (1996). The role of neighbors and the government in neighborhood-based child protection. *Journal of Social Issues, 52*(3), 163–176.

Latting, J.K., & Blanchard, A. (1997). Empowering staff in a 'poverty agency': An organization development intervention. *Journal of Community Practice, 4*(3), 59–75.

Leon, A.M. (1999). Family support model: Integrating service delivery in the twenty-first century. *Families in Society, 80*(1), 14–24.

Leong, F.T., & Zachar, P. (1991). Development and validation of the scientist-practitioner inventory for psychology. *Journal of Counseling Psychology, 38*(3), 331–341.

Leukefeld, C.G. (1990, August 3). National health line. *Health and Social Work, 15*, 175–179.

Lord, B., & Pockett, R. (1998). Perceptions of social work intervention with bereaved clients: Some implications for hospital social work practice. *Social Work in Health Care, 27*(1), 51–66.

MacEachron, A.E., & Gustavsson, N.S. (1997, November/December). Reframing practitioner research. *Families in Society: The Journal of Contemporary Human Services, 78*(6) 651–656.

Manthey, M. (2001). Reflective practice. *Creative Nursing, 7*(2), 3–5.

Martin, L.M., Peters, C.L., & Glisson, C. (1998). Factors affecting case management recommendations for children entering state custody. *Social Service Review, 72*(4), 521–544.

Masson, H., & Morrison, T. (1991). A 24 hour duty system: Using practitioner research to manage the stress. *British Journal of Social Work, 21*, 361–372.

Measelle, J.R., Weinstein, R.S., & Martinez, M. (1998). Parent satisfaction with case managed systems of care for children and youth with severe emotional disturbances. *Journal of Child and Family Studies, 7*(4), 451–467.

Mellor, J.M., & Lindeman, D. (1998). The role of the social worker in interdisciplinary geriatric teams. *Journal of Gerontological Social Work, 30*(3/4), 3–7.

Ministry of Children and Family Development (2002). *Integrated case management training modules.* Victoria, BC: Government of British Columbia.

Munro, E. (1999). Common errors of reasoning in child protection work. *Child Abuse & Neglect, 23*(8), 745–758.

Murray, R., McKay, E., Thompson, S., & Donald, M. (2000). Practising reflection: A medical humanities approach to occupational therapist education. *Medical Teacher, 22*(3), 276–282.

Nelson, P., McCulloch, L., & Clague, M. (1995). *Making Partnerships Work: A Review of the Management Models of 14 Interministerial Programs in Vancouver.* Report prepared for the Vancouver Regional Child and Youth Committee. Vancouver, BC, Canada.

Netting, E.F., & Williams, F.G. (1999, March 1). Implementing a case management program designed to enhance primary care physician practice with older persons. *The Journal of Applied Gerontology, 18*, 25–45.

Nexus Residential Program. (no date). *Case management: Nexus observation and intervention program.* Kentville, N.S.: Western Region Case Management Committee, Department of Community Services.

O'Looney, J. (1994). Modeling collaboration and social services integration: A single state's experience with developmental and non-developmental models. *Administration in Social Work, 18*(1), 61–86.

Ovretveit, J. (1993). *Coordinating community care: Multidisciplinary teams and case management.* Bristol, PA: Open University Press.

Paget, T. (2001). Reflective practice and clinical outcomes: Practitioners views. *Journal of Clinical Nursing, 10*(2), 204–215.

Powell-Stanard, R. (1999, April 2). The effect of training in a strengths model of case management on client outcomes in a community mental health center. *Community Mental Health Journal, 35*, 169–179.

Prochaska, J.O., Norcross, J.C., & DiClemente, C.C. (1994). *Changing for good.* New York: William Morrow & Company.

Ransohoff, J. (1994, September/October). Probing the "mystery" of behavioral case management. *Behavioral Health Management, 14*(5) 29–30.

Ricks, F. (1991a). *Accountability case management* (3rd ed.). Victoria, BC: Author.

Ricks, F. (1991b, August). The complexities of family assessment. *The Clinical Counsellor,* 48–57.

Ricks, F., & Griffin, S. (1995). *Best choice: Ethical decision-making in human services practice.* Victoria, BC: Ministry of Skills, Training and Labour.

Ricks, F., & Marks, J. (1997). I'm not a researcher but.; *Journal of Cooperative Education, XXXII,* 46–54.

Ricks, F., Charlesworth, J., Bellefeuille, G., & Field, A. (1999). *All together now: Creating a social capital mosaic.* Victoria, BC: F. Ricks and the Vanier Institute of the Family.

Rindfleisch, N., & Hicho, D. (1987, July/August 4). Institutional child protection: Issues in program development and implementation. *Child Welfare, LXVI,* 329–342.

Roberts-DeGennaro, M. (1987, October). Developing case management as a practice model. *Social Casework: The Journal of Contemporary Social Work, 68*(8) 466–470.

Rogers, C.R. (1955). A personal view of some issues facing psychologists. *American Psychologist, 10,* 247–249.

Rutman, D., Hubberstey, C., Hume, S., & Tate, B. (1998). *Review of integrated case management.* Victoria, BC: Child, Family and Community Research Program, University of Victoria.

Saunders, E.J., & Goodall, K. (1985, November/December 6). A social services-public health partnership in child protection: A rural model. *Public Health Reports, 100,* 663–666.

Savell, K.S., Huston, A.D., & Malkin, M.J. (1993). Collaborative research: Bridging the gap between practitioners and researchers/educators. In M. Malkin and C. Howe (Eds.) *Research in therapeutic recreation: Concepts and methods.* State College, PA: Venture Publishing, Inc.

Scannapieco, M., & Hegar, R.L. (1994, August 4). Kinship care: Two case models. *Child and Adolescent Social Work Journal, 11,* 315–324.

Schon, D.A. (1983). *The reflective practitioner.* New York: Basic Books.

Skehill, C., O'Sullivan, E., & Buckley, H. (2000, May). The nature of child protection practices: An Irish case study. *Child and Family Social Work, 4,* 145–152.

Skilling, K. (2001). It's time to reflect on the benefits of reflective practice! *Primary Educator, 7*(3), 7–12.

Solomon, P., & Draine, J. (1994, April 2). Family perceptions of consumers as case managers. *Community Mental Health Journal, 30,* 165–176.

Staats, A. (1993, January). Redefinitions of the science-practice relationship without a framework for unity will fail. *American Psychologist, 48*(1) 58–67.

Swets, R., Rutman, D., & Wharf, B. (1996). *The community development initiative: A review of the experience and a framework for practice.* Victoria, BC: Child, Family and Community Research Program, University of Victoria.

Tinsley, E., Tinsley, H., Boone, S., & Shim-Li, C. (1993). Prediction of scientist-practitioner behavior using personality scores obtained during graduate school. *Journal of Counseling Psychology, 40*(4), 511–517.

Van Gyn, G.H. (1996). Reflective practice: The needs of professions and the promise of cooperative education. *Journal of Cooperative Education, 31*(2–3), 103–131.

Walton, E., & Smith, C. (1999). Intervention in child welfare: The genogram as a tool for assessment. *Journal of Family Social Work, 3*(3), 3–20.

Weingart, P. & Stehr, N. (2000). *Practising Interdisciplinarity.* Toronto, ON: University of Toronto Press.

Werrbach, G.B. (1994, August 2). Intensive child case management: Work roles and activities. *Child and Adolescent Social Work Journal, 11*, 325–341.

Yennie, H. (1997, March/April). Utilization and case management software. *Behavioral Health Management, 17*, 8–10.

Index

CPSIA information can be obtained at www.ICGtesting.com
Printed in the USA
LVOW050139200911

247022LV00005B/7/A